GROWING VEGETABLES IN HAWAI'I

A How-to Guide for the Gardener

KATHY OSHIRO

THE BESS PRESS

3565 Harding Ave. Honolulu, Hawai'i 96816 • Phone (808) 734-7159 • Fax (808) 732-3627
www.besspress.com

To my mother, who taught me the joys and attributes of getting my hands dirty in the soil, and who always used to say: "Eat your vegetables!" Thanks for everything, Mother. We miss you.

Design and cover: Carol Colbath
Photo on page 23 courtesy of Quindembo Bamboo Nursery

Library of Congress Cataloging-in-Publication Data

Oshiro, Kathy.
    Growing vegetables in Hawaii : a how-to guide
for the gardener / Kathy Oshiro.
          p.   cm.
    ISBN 1-57306-080-1
    1. Vegetable gardening - Hawaii. 2. Native plant
gardening - Hawaii. 3. Tropical vegetables - Hawaii.
4. Gardening - Hawaii. I. Title.
SB324.56.H3.083 1999   635.9'51969-dc20

Printed in Korea

CONTENTS

Note: Although artichokes, breadfruit, shallots, and tomatoes are classified as fruits or herbs, they are included in this book because they are commonly prepared as vegetables.

INTRODUCTION

"Begin planting when all signs of frost are gone and you are able to work the soil." Yes, I too got tired of reading this type of advice in the gardening books I pulled from the bookshelf, looking for help with my Hawai'i garden. And just try to find a book that tells you how to grow breadfruit or taro! Even if you have a book on growing pipinola or daikon, how do you prepare it after you grow it?

I love to cook and had always wanted to write a cookbook. But everyone and his or her auntie has done that. Seeing the need for a gardening book specific to Hawai'i, I decided to write one that also includes recipes. My initial project evolved into two books: the one you're holding now, *Growing Vegetables in Hawai'i*, and a companion volume, *Growing Fruits, Herbs, Nuts, and Seeds in Hawai'i*. Both are designed to encourage gardeners to grow a variety of produce easily transformed into delicious, nutritious meals.

The gardening advice in this book is based largely on my experience living in three different areas of Hawai'i, all with very different soils and weather conditions, requiring adjustments and variations in gardening techniques. Use this book as a guide and don't be afraid to experiment.

And don't get discouraged! Sometimes we had nothing growing in our garden but green onions and weeds. But, boy, when we finally decided to get our garden going again, how nice it was to smell the green onions when we brushed against them as we pulled those weeds!

Enjoy your garden, and eat your vegetables!

ACKNOWLEDGMENTS

As someone who would rather be outside pulling weeds than confined in the house doing detail work, there is no way I could have written this book without the support and understanding of my husband and three daughters. They were patient when all my accumulated research and reference books were scattered throughout the house. They were even more patient when dinner was often late because I had "just one more paragraph" to finish. Add to that their help with the household chores when writing about vegetables became so much more important to me than doing the laundry or dishes. Thank you for being there, above and beyond the call of duty.

Specific thank yous to my husband, Glenn, for his advice, comments, and suggestions and for keeping our own garden alive while I spent all my time just writing about it; our daughter Kimberly, whose diligent assistance in starting our new garden on the Big Island in the mud and mist made me determined to learn how to garden successfully in less than desirable conditions, and live to write about it; our daughter Margot, for not only helping me to learn to use the computer, but also taking care of all those dirty dishes; and finally, our daughter Heather. Although she is the last person one would find in a garden, her excelling at the University of Hawai'i-Mānoa and desire to be published herself inspired me to be first! Thanks, kiddo.

Thank you to my father, too, for giving me the opportunity to grow up on an acre and experience "country living" for my first nineteen years.

A major mahalo to Peter Berg and Susan Ruskin, owners of Quindembo Bamboo Nursery, without whose kind help and advice there would be no bamboo entry in this book.

I could not have written this book without the guidance and technical support I received from the dedicated personnel at the University of Hawai'i Extension Service of Kamuela. And many thanks to Norman Bezona, Professor Emeritus, University of Hawai'i College of Tropical Agriculture and Human Resources, for his advice and encouragement.

ardening should be an enjoyable and rewarding experience, not a chore. This book is designed to help the Hawai'i backyard gardener grow vegetables as successfully as possible. However, the advice in this book does not have to be followed to the letter to ensure success. If you miss an application—or two—of fertilizer, do not panic. Your plants will still thrive. If you don't want to mulch your plants, fine. You will probably still have a successful crop.

Do not be afraid to experiment. Adjust. Alter. Talk to friends, neighbors. Just be sure to enjoy yourself. To help you enjoy the rewards of harvesting your first flavorful bounty, the section on growing each vegetable includes two simple but delicious recipes.

SOIL AND FERTILIZERS

Soil is more than dirt. It provides a medium in which plants can anchor their roots; it stores water, air, and nutrients—elements necessary for all plant life. Therefore, the better your soil is, the healthier your plants will be.

Different areas of Hawai'i vary greatly in soil composition. In younger areas, only several layers of organic matter lie atop either 'a'ā or pāhoehoe. If the organic matter lies atop pāhoehoe, the area will have no drainage, whereas if it lies atop 'a'ā there will be good drainage. Knowing the soil composition of your area will help you determine what may or may not need to be added to your garden plot.

Organic matter, the decaying remains of dead plants and animals, is essential for fertile soil. Organic matter aerates the soil and helps it retain water. Water retention not only ensures that water will be available for the plants themselves, but also dissolves nutrients in the soil and, by keeping the soil moist, allows the nutrients to stay in the soil longer. The addition of organic material also improves the soil's texture, which in turn encourages healthy root growth and a healthier plant.

Plants need nutrients in order to grow. They get these nutrients from the soil. Some plants, like corn, take more nutrients than others and are rightly called "heavy feeders."

The nutrients plants need are nitrogen, phosphorus, and potassium. Plants also need trace elements, such as salt and calcium.

Nitrogen is needed heavily by plants grown primarily for their leaves, like lettuce, chard, and cabbage. Too much nitrogen in other vegetables can cause the plant to produce more and more leaves, causing slow blossoming and fruit bearing. Good sources of nitrogen are blood meal, fish scraps, and bone meal.

Phosphorus promotes fruit production and the production of healthy root systems. Good sources of phosphorus are bone meal, fish scraps, and cottonseed meal.

Potassium promotes leaf and stem growth. It also helps the plant take in other nutrients. Greens, macadamia nut husks, coffee cherry shells, banana peels, granite meal, and potash nitrate are good sources of potassium.

Commercial fertilizers are labeled according to their proportionate amounts of nitrogen, phosphorus, and potassium, in that order. A general, all-purpose fertilizer labeled 10-30-10 (equal amounts of nitrogen and potassium and heavy amounts of phosphorus)—or 10-20-20 when plants require more potassium—is usually suitable for vegetable gardening here in Hawai'i. Trace elements should also be present in a complete fertilizer.

When possible, use organic fertilizers and organic materials. Commercial fertilizers should be used sparingly. Too much fertilizer can do more harm than good, so be careful not to overdose the garden. Commercial fertilizers contain salts that accumulate in the soil over the years. Too much salt in your soil may severely restrict the germination, growth, and yield of most vegetable plants.

Instead of depending heavily on commercial fertilizers, improve the overall health of your garden soil by consistently adding natural elements, such as rotted manure and compost.

MANURE TEA

A highly effective and inexpensive way to fertilize plants is with a mixture you can make yourself called manure tea. During the plantation days in Hawai'i, folks applied chicken manure directly to their vegetable gardens, as the vegetable plants were growing. The risk of this practice, however, was overdosing the plants, causing nitrogen burns. Manure tea is a safe, effective alternative.

The best manures to use, in order of effectiveness, are chicken, rabbit, sheep, steer, and horse. You may be able to obtain animal manures from local farmers, stables, feedlots, or even zoos. Dried, bagged manure is now available at most local garden shops. Do not use dog or cat manure. These manures may carry diseases that can be transmitted to humans.

To make manure tea, put a few shovelfuls (or use a coffee can instead of a shovel) of either fresh or dried manure into a burlap or plastic mesh feed bag. (The bag should be permeable, but with very fine holes.) Tie the bag closed. Place your newly made "tea bag" into a large bucket or other container filled with water. Be sure the bag is completely submerged. After your "tea" has steeped for about 1 week, it is ready to use.

Use the manure tea full strength in place of commercial fertilizer when feeding your vegetables. Or dilute and use every time you water. Experiment with the amount of water you use to dilute, starting with a formula of 5 parts water to 1 part manure tea.

After use, put what remains of the "tea bag" in your compost pile.

THE COMPOST PILE

The addition of organic material to soil is essential. You can obtain such organic material by buying bags of compost at your local garden supply store, but this is quite costly. It is less expensive to make your own compost from materials you would have otherwise thrown away or hauled to the dump. If my sister-in-law, who lives in the suburbs of Los Angeles, makes her own compost, you can do it too!

Your style of compost-making will be dictated by the amount of yard space you have, as well as by your own personal preferences. When I was a child we simply had a "compost pile": just plant waste, piled high. It was probably 4 feet high, 4 feet wide, and 12 feet long and was great fun to run up and down on! When we needed fertilizer, we just dug from the bottom of the pile to remove some of the beautiful, soft, fluffy mixture that had been produced over a period of months and months.

Today, compost-making by the home gardener is much more efficient. If you put your dead plant mixture in a container or bin instead of just a pile, you will be able to more easily turn and mix the contents, speeding decomposition.

You can make your compost bin out of a variety of materials: wire mesh, concrete blocks, wooden slats. Anything that allows air to penetrate from the sides is best.

Place garden debris, grass clippings, leaves, manure, and small twigs in your bin. The smaller the debris, the faster it will decompose. You can also add kitchen scraps and refuse, including coffee grounds. However, egg shells and meat scraps, although fine to use in your compost, may attract mice and rats. You may therefore wish to exclude these from your compost.

Water the pile and cover with heavy plastic, if you wish. Covering helps retain moisture and heat, speeding decomposition.

Turn the contents of your compost bin weekly, if possible. It is not essential to turn the compost pile frequently; your compost will just not decompose quite as fast if you don't. Keep the material watered, so it is as damp as a squeezed-out sponge.

Continue to add garden debris and scraps. Adding a cup or two of 10-30-10 fertilizer to each large load will help speed decomposition. Build your pile until it is 3 to 4 feet high. Then turn, water, cover with heavy plastic, and start a new bin. Turn your first compost pile, weekly if possible, until it is entirely crumbly, blackish matter with "unrecognizable" contents. Your compost is now ready to add to your garden.

Don't worry about missing steps. These techniques for compost-making only speed up what nature does anyway. You really cannot ruin a compost heap!

GARDEN AND SOIL PREPARATION

If you are looking for the single most important element to a successful garden, soil preparation is probably it. But like cooking, gardening is more an art than an exact science, so treat it as such. There is no truly "perfect" soil, but rather a range of soil conditions and compositions that make a vegetable garden productive.

pH

Soils are either acid, neutral, or alkaline. How acidic or alkaline a soil happens to be is measured by a numeric symbol called pH. The pH scale ranges from 0 (acid) to 14 (alkaline), with the number 7 being the neutral point. Unlike soils of much of the U.S. mainland, soils in Hawai'i are acidic, which is common for areas with high rainfall. Note that the drier sides of the islands may be more alkaline, as well as higher in calcium and salts. However, rather than try to correct your soil to a perfect 7.0 pH, aim for a pH range of 6.5 to 7.5. Such a pH range enables you to successfully grow a wider variety of plants, because some vegetables prefer a more alkaline soil, and some a more acid one.

SITE SELECTION

Select a fairly level area for your garden. If a large enough level area is not available, consider either terracing a sloping area or making several long, narrow terraces in your yard to accommodate your plants. If you live in a condo or in a high-wind area, consider gardening in containers on your lanai. Many vegetables do beautifully grown in containers, given a bit of extra care and attention.

The area selected should be in full sun and away from trees as much as possible. Trees provide unwanted shade, and their roots tend to reach out far beyond their own area, robbing any nearby garden plants of needed soil nutrients. Try to select a garden area that can take advantage of the morning sun as well as the afternoon sun. Your garden plot should also be as protected from winds as possible. And, of course, be sure to have a good water source nearby.

SOIL PREPARATION

Mark out your garden area. Then, using a shovel, turn over the soil of the entire area, removing all weeds and other vegetation as you go along. Then go back and, using a garden fork, work the entire garden, digging and turning over the soil to a depth of 8 to 12 inches. Be sure to remove as many rocks and pebbles as possible.

SOIL SAMPLE

At this point you should stop and collect a soil sample. Then, contact your local U. H. College of Tropical Agriculture and Human Resources (CTAHR) to obtain instructions on how to obtain a soil analysis. For a nominal fee the CTAHR will not only tell you the pH range in your garden but will also give you advice on how to bring it to the pH range you desire.

Soil testing is also available from mainland companies. Although their test results may be faster, they may also be more expensive.

While you are waiting for the soil sample analysis, your garden plot will have a chance to "rest." This rest benefits the soil, especially in areas that have not previously been used for gardening. Perhaps the tilling and resting process allows air, an essential element of healthy soil, to be mixed throughout the plot.

Your CTAHR soil analysis report will probably recommend adding lime (crushed coral or dolomite) to your soil to make the soil less acidic. Dolomite, which is a mixture of minerals, primarily calcium and magnesium carbonate, is preferable, since using too much crushed coral (which is only calcium carbonate) may actually poison your soil without adding the correct balance of other necessary accompanying minerals like magnesium. Note, however, that using too much of either dolomite or crushed coral may overcorrect the soil, making it too alkaline.

Apply dolomite to your garden area in the amounts recommended on your soil sample report and work it into the soil.

If you have compost or animal manure, this is the time to dig it into your soil. Note: Do not use dog or cat manure. These may contain diseases that can be transmitted to humans.

Important note: Be sure to mention in your report request the crop you plan to plant, as well as the size of the area to be planted. Otherwise, your soil sample report will probably tell you the amount of dolomite or other material to use per acre, e. g., "add 1,000 pounds dolomite per one acre of garden space." You will have to convert this information to a more usable square-foot application. To do this, devise a formula, knowing that an acre contains 43,560 square feet and a pound has 16 ounces. Remember that "ounces," used here, is a measure of weight, not a measure of volume. Therefore, 2 ounces of dolomite does not mean $1/4$ cup! You will have to weigh each particular chemical to determine how much an ounce is in volume. Consider purchasing an inexpensive kitchen scale to weigh your chemicals. It also helps to write the measurement equivalent, or proportion needed, on each chemical package when you first make the calculation, so you will not have to do the math every time you want to use it.

PLANT SELECTION AND ARRANGEMENT

Level your garden plot as much as possible, or terrace if necessary. Plan what vegetables you wish to plant, taking into consideration 1) plant height at maturity (some plants cause shade); 2) how long the vegetable takes to grow from planting to harvest (some take 30 days total, some 4 or more months); 3) whether your plant is a permanent one that will remain in the garden for several years (some herbs, asparagus, etc.).

After you have decided what you want to plant, where you want to plant it, and how much area each specific vegetable will require (see the individual plant descriptions in this book for information helpful in making these decisions), lay out your garden plot, being sure to 1) make room for walkways, so you can get to the various garden areas; and 2) make each individual garden area only large enough for you to be able to reach around it from the walkways. When you are planting, weeding, and harvesting, you don't want to have to step into the individual garden plots, since this compacts the soil and hinders growth. If you terrace your garden, the terraces help define walkways, and the raised beds make bending over a little easier.

SEED AND PLANT SELECTION

SPECIAL CONDITIONS

Seeds and seedlings are readily available at local nursery and grocery stores and from mail order catalogs. Before you buy seeds or seedlings, however, remember that Hawai'i has its own unique climates, soils, and growing conditions. Seeds that do well in most areas of the mainland may not thrive here in Hawai'i.

For one thing, we have no harsh winters to destroy some pests and diseases. Our humid air causes problems unknown to plants in drier climates. In addition, our soils tend to be highly acidic because of the volcanoes. (In fact, our soils are not only different from those on the mainland, but also vary throughout the islands: we have porous lava-rock soils, sandy soils, loamy soils, and heavy clay soils.) We also have varying climates throughout our state. Although we are in a tropical zone, our mountainous islands and deep surrounding ocean produce cooler weather than that found in other tropical areas. Consider all this, plus the changes in elevation and rainfall patterns throughout the islands, when planning and tending your Hawai'i garden. Select your vegetables for planting accordingly. (But don't be afraid to experiment, too!)

SEEDS AND SEEDLINGS

Whenever possible, the Hawai'i gardener should buy seeds that have been specially developed for growing in our islands. For example, corn reacts to temperatures and day length. We don't have the long summer days of the mainland. If you use mainland corn varieties your crop will have stunted growth and tiny ears. Because of our state's unique conditions, the University of Hawai'i has spent years developing special varieties of seeds that are resistant to Hawai'i pests and diseases. Use of such seeds will help ensure a successful harvest.

Buying seedlings locally offers similar advantages. Local nurseries usually stock only varieties that do well in Hawai'i. Consider the reasons your local nursery has for not stocking a particular variety before you decide to obtain it elsewhere.

For your convenience, this book includes an island-by-island list of local nurseries where you can find plants mentioned in this book (page 90) and information for requesting a CTAHR Seed Order Form (page 89).

At times you may wish to experiment with other vegetables, or specific varieties, not specifically developed for Hawai'i. Therefore, also included in the back of this book, under Suppliers, are addresses for ordering mainland seed catalogs. Note that some seeds developed and marketed in Japan may do well here in Hawai'i.

But for the best overall success in your Hawai'i backyard garden, stick to those seeds and plants especially adapted to our state. And, when deciding exactly WHAT to plant, be sure to take into consideration the tastes of your family. No sense in having a bountiful crop of bittermelon if no one in your family will eat it!

How much should you plant? It depends on the size of your vegetable garden, and of course, how much you like a particular vegetable. The time of year, your geographical location within the islands, and the quality of your soil will all play a big part in how much a particular plant will bear. Only experience, however, will let you know if you have planted enough snow peas, for example, to satisfy your family or to feed an army. But remember, an overabundance of vegetables supplies you with wonderful gifts for friends and neighbors. And, when you have been blessed with too many tomatoes, or too many eggplant, consider donating the excess to your local food bank.

WHEN TO PLANT

One of the wonderful advantages of gardening in Hawai'i is that we do not have severe winters or snow that will kill our precious crops. Therefore, we have the opportunity to plant many different vegetables all year long. Some, however, will do better if planted during certain times of the year, so refer to the chart below for guidance when determining when to plant.

Remember, however, that different areas in Hawai'i vary greatly when it comes to temperature, rainfall, and soil conditions. I encourage you to experiment with your planting to find out just how a particular vegetable will do "out of season." For example, it is recommended that you plant corn in the spring or summer. But last year we planted a small crop of corn in the late fall, and it ripened in winter. Granted, we only had a 10% pollinization rate, rather than our usual 90% rate, but it was sure wonderful to have those few tender ears of corn for a couple of winter meals. So, experiment; you really have nothing to lose but a bit of time, and a few seeds.

	SPRING (March-May)	SUMMER (June-August)	FALL (Sept.-Nov.)	WINTER (Dec.-Feb.)
Aloe	●	●	●	●
Artichokes				●
Arugula	●			●
Asparagus	●			●
Bamboo	●	●	●	●
Beans	●	●	●	●
Beets	●	●	●	●
Bittermelon	●	●	●	●
Breadfruit	●	●	●	●
Broccoli	●		●	●
Brussels sprouts			●	
Cabbage				●
Carrots	●	●	●	●
Cauliflower				
Chinese cabbage				●
Chinese peas			●	●
Corn	●	●		
Cucumbers	●	●	●	●
Daikon	●	●	●	●
Eggplant	●	●	●	●
Green onions and chives	●	●	●	●
Lettuce	●		●	●
Onions	●	●	●	●
Peas			●	●
Peppers	●	●	●	●
Pipinola	●	●	●	●
Potatoes	●	●	●	●
Radish	●	●	●	●
Shallots				●
Spinach				●
Squash	●	●		
Sweet potatoes	●	●	●	●
Swiss chard	●	●	●	●
Taro	●	●	●	●
Tomatoes	●	●	●	●
Watercress	●	●	●	●

HAWAIIAN MOON CALENDAR

The Ancient Hawaiian Moon Calendar is based on a theory similar to that of the Old Farmers' Almanac: planting by the phases of the moon can affect the success or failure of crops. Ancient Hawaiians planted all their crops in correlation with the different phases of the moon. They also reserved certain days each month for worship.

Each day of the Hawaiian lunar month had a different name, unlike the mainland method of referring to only four quarters. Thus, the ancient Hawaiians were able to be more specific about when to plant, and when not to plant, certain crops. But the ancient Hawaiians were not idle during those moon phases thought to be unproductive for planting and harvesting; those "unproductive" days were the days reserved for weeding, fishing, chores, or prayer.

Today, many local farmers still plant crops according to the moon's phases. They believe the full moon (Māhealani) is a great time to plant sweet potatoes and taro, whereas the last phase, the dark night with no moon, or new moon (Muku) is not. Lā'aukūlua, roughly the beginning of the last quarter, is a good day to plant anything but vines; and 'Olekūkolu, near the end of the first quarter, is a day totally unproductive for any planting.

You may want to pick up a Hawaiian Moon Calendar (which also has a fishing guide), experiment with its suggestions, and perhaps benefit from the knowledge acquired over the centuries. You can buy the annual Hawaiian Moon Calendar through the Prince Kūhiō Hawaiian Civic Club (their address is listed under Suppliers, page 91) or at bookstores throughout Hawai'i.

IMPATIENT (HARVEST NOW) VS. PATIENT (WAIT A WHILE) VEGETABLES

One of the reasons you may have decided to have your own garden is that you want the highest quality, best-tasting vegetables available. Many vegetables lose their quality and flavor by the time they reach the local supermarket. Some homegrown vegetables, too, can lose quality and flavor if not harvested promptly.

To take advantage of the freshness homegrown vegetables can offer, it is important to know which ones require immediate attention when they are ready to be harvested ("impatient" vegetables), and which ones can be "patient." Impatient vegetables must be harvested immediately, sometimes not waiting one extra day, or they will lose their peak fresh flavor and texture. Patient vegetables can wait days, even weeks, to be harvested after they are ripe and still retain most of their quality.

Impatient vegetables include asparagus, corn, Chinese peas, and cucumbers. Patient vegetables include beets, carrots, onions, potatoes, radishes, sweet potatoes, and Swiss chard.

FENCES AND TRELLISES

When planning your garden, consider your surroundings and your neighborhood. If there are dogs or cats in the area, it makes sense to put a fence around your garden. A simple, inexpensive fence made of mesh wire or chicken wire will help you avoid the disappointment of coming out one morning to see paw prints where your lettuce seedlings used to be, and a happy dog or cat nearby!

If you have a fence around your garden and are planning to have climbing vegetables, like Chinese peas and cucumbers, plant them next to the fence. Then you will not need additional plant supports or trellises.

Should your plants (Chinese peas, cucumbers, some tomatoes and beans) need support while growing, the supports need not be expensive or elaborate. You can buy fancy trellises from your garden supply store. However, you can also use dried limbs, either alone or tied with kite string, to make a simple trellis.

Kite string (or knitting yarn) strung between two sticks zig-zag style makes a great support for Chinese peas or cucumbers. So does old fishing line. But remember that whatever you use should be cleaned up after harvest, since you do not want plastic or slow-rotting yarn in your compost.

For tomatoes, try using the wire used for support in concrete foundations. This wire usually comes in 4-foot widths and is much more durable than the ready-made tomato cages found at the store. Cut it in 5-foot lengths and bend it to make a "cage." Cut the first horizontal wire off at the bottom, leaving vertical "feet." Push the "feet" into the ground around each tomato plant to secure the cage.

DECORATIVE AND CONTAINER GARDENING

No room for a garden? Consider making vegetables part of your landscaping. Plant climbing vegetables, such as snow peas, tomatoes, or cucumbers, next to your decorative trellises. Landscape with decorative vegetables such as asparagus; or line the outside perimeter of a flower garden with Mānoa lettuce.

If you have an outdoor lanai, you have room to grow vegetables. Or line walkways with decorative containers planted with a variety of vegetables. Several vegetables do beautifully grown in small, medium, or large containers. Try beets, carrots, Chinese snow peas, cucumbers, eggplant, lettuce, peppers, potatoes, radishes, and tomatoes.

Use your imagination when choosing containers for your mini–vegetable garden. Many commercially made wooden and plastic containers are available. Or consider using old kitchen pots, plastic hampers, or clay pots. (Remember that you will need to add drainage holes to any solid containers you use.)

Use a commercial planting mix. Regular garden soil is too dense for successful plant growth in a container. The soils for containers need to have high water-retention ability, so a combination of peat moss, perlite, vermiculite, and well-rotted compost is recommended.

Do not fill containers completely with planting soil. Leave enough space at the top of the container to allow for watering. Plant seeds and seedlings in containers using the same methods you would use in the garden.

Water thoroughly, when needed. Be sure not to let the containers completely dry out, because it will be very difficult to re-wet the soil. You will need to water your containers more often than a garden plot since container soil and plants cannot soak up moisture from the water table like topsoil in the garden can. On hotter days, you may need to water your containers more than once. A simple way to determine if you need to water is by scratching the top of the soil with your finger. If the soil is dry beneath the surface, you need to water. If you use a water softener for your household water, use water from an outside tap to water your containers. Many water softeners contain sodium, which is harmful to your plants.

Fertilize your container gardens with a balanced, time-release dry or liquid fertilizer or manure tea. Watch your plant growth, and its coloration, to determine if and when more fertilizer is needed, since container gardening requires more input of nutrients than regular vegetable gardening.

Watering

You already know that plants will not survive without water, but how you water is important also.

Weather conditions help determine how often you should water. Warm sun and windy weather dry the soil quickly. And, of course, rainfall amounts and frequency are important factors to consider when you are determining how often to water your garden.

Observe your garden. Pull up a weed and see if the soil that clings to the roots is moist. Although the top of the soil may be dry, the soil below may still have sufficient moisture. Remember that too much water can rot the plants, as well as wash away important soil nutrients.

Some plants, like lettuce, require more water than others, so you may find yourself watering certain portions of the garden on a frequent basis, other portions perhaps weekly.

How much is enough? Hawai'i ranchers use the following gauge: take a handful of soil and squeeze. If it drips water or turns to mud it's saturated. If it balls up and then falls apart when you put it down it's ideal. And if it doesn't hold together at all, you have a drought.

When watering seedbeds or young seedlings, use a very gentle spray. Try to imitate a gentle rain. A heavy spray from the hose can dig up and disrupt your seedbed or break the leaves of young seedlings.

Whenever possible, water in the early morning, before the hot sun begins to beat down. Water well, and deeply. A thorough, deep watering is better than a few frequent light sprinkles, since a light sprinkle may cause the top of the soil to become hard and crusty. In extremely sun-intensive areas you may consider using a shade cloth over your vegetables, especially young transplants, to keep them from wilting. If possible, use locally available plant shelters, like old palm fronds and bamboo, to build a shelter for your delicate plants.

In the full-sun areas of Hawai'i, like Lahaina and Kailua-Kona, consider using shade cloth (available at hardware stores and nurseries) to keep plants (especially young transplants) from wilting during the summer months. These shade cloths help the plants and soil avoid excessive water loss. Mulching around your plants with grass clippings, hay, straw, dried leaves, or other mulching material also helps soil retain moisture.

Watering in the midafternoon may be necessary for young seedlings recently transplanted. As a general rule, try to avoid watering the leaves of the plants; instead, water low, next to the stems. This prevents pounding delicate leaves with water drops and damaging them. Avoid watering in the late afternoon or evening, since water on the leaves will not have a chance to dry, attracting insects and causing mold and rot.

With a little common sense and a bit of experience, you will soon establish your own successful watering system.

Pest Control

Hawai'i has a subtropical climate that allows us to garden all year long, with no cold weather and frosts to destroy our crops. However, we also do not have cold weather and frosts to destroy unwanted insects. Therefore, we must accept the fact that pests exist, and learn to garden in spite of their existence.

Before dealing with pests, consider that perhaps one of the reasons you wanted to grow your own vegetables was to have some control over the amount of pesticides used on what you eat. Commercial fruits and vegetables are saturated with potent pesticides. In fact, many pesticides used by commercial growers are so potent that they are not available for use by the general public. Remember then, that not only are you in control of the amount of pesticides that end up on your homegrown vegetables, but you can also be assured that whatever pesticides you do use are probably less harmful to your body than those commercial chemicals used on "store-bought" foods.

Since we do not know for certain the effects of pesticide use on health, avoid pesticide use as much as possible, and then, when you do use pesticides, use them sparingly and follow the label instructions meticulously. Throughout this book, I will frequently warn you to USE EXTREME CARE WHEN USING PESTICIDES AND READ AND FOLLOW PACKAGE INSTRUCTIONS AND WARNINGS CAREFULLY. This includes making sure the crop you plan to use the pesticide on is a crop listed on the pesticide package.

When using chemical preparations, use sparingly and with caution. Read label directions carefully, taking into consideration your planned harvest date, as well as the harvest date of the surrounding plants. Remember, if you use a toxic insecticide to control a pest, you may also risk killing "friendly" insects, those that naturally control the destructive pests.

Brand names, such as Diazinon and Sevin, are used in this book simply for ease of reference, not as endorsements of those particular product brands. Generic products that contain the same chemicals work just as successfully against pests as do the name brands, and are less expensive.

Using organic gardening methods is one way to deal with pests. The techniques used in organic gardening are a "natural" way of combating pests, and I highly encourage using these techniques.

To control pests using organic gardening methods, try the following:

- Use only seed varieties developed by the University of Hawai'i. These seeds were developed to resist many pests and diseases known in Hawai'i.

- If buying seedlings from your local nursery, choose only healthy plants; they attract fewer pests.

- Keep your garden free of weeds, which give pests a place to hide and breed. After a crop is finished, remove all plant debris from the garden.

- Do not water leaves of plants in the afternoon or evening.

- Put out small pans, or tuna cans, buried so the top of the container is even with the soil surface. Fill with a small amount of beer. Stale beer attracts slugs, who fall into the container and drown. Change the beer daily. (My husband says it's a waste of good beer, but it works!)

- Handpick larger pests from plants and soil and place in a bucket containing soapy water. This works especially well in controlling Chinese rose beetles, corn worms, and cutworms. Be sure to check your garden for pests at night as well as during the day.

- Hose or wash off aphids when you first notice them on your plants.

- Plant more than you actually need, allowing for a percentage of your crop to be damaged—with enough left for a satisfying harvest.

- Use nonchemical preparations, such as insecticidal soaps, which paralyze insects, causing them to starve to death; natural pyrethrins (from dried daisy flowers), which attack the insects' central nervous system; and horticultural oils, which you can buy at your local nursery, or even make at home.

Recipes for homemade preparations can be found in any organic gardening book. Note, however, that some of these nonchemical mixtures may have to be used more often than the chemical mixtures in order to be effective. One such recipe is for cigarette tea: soak old cigarette butts in water for several days. Use in a spray bottle as an insecticide, taking care, however, that the solution is not too concentrated.

Avid organic gardeners suggest planting pest deterrents among your vegetable crops, such as

beans or marigolds among potatoes, to discourage potato beetles

catnip, mint, rosemary, sage, or thyme among any cabbage plants, to repel the white cabbage moth

chives or garlic among lettuce and peas, to deter aphids

marigolds among beans, to repel beetles

nasturtiums throughout your garden, to discourage aphids, beetles, and squash bugs

potatoes with beans, to discourage bean beetles

radishes among cucumbers, to discourage cucumber beetles

tomatoes with asparagus, to discourage asparagus beetles

Another way to deal with pests is to avoid plants that attract pests. If you have to struggle repeatedly to keep pests off eggplant, for example, simply consider not growing these in your garden. With a little bit of patience and experimentation, you will be able to determine which plants will grow easily and successfully in your garden with little or no pesticide use.

In Hawai'i, our main pests are aphids, cutworms, mites (spider mites), whiteflies and fruit flies, white moths, slugs, grasshoppers, and—able to destroy a vegetable garden in spite of their size—the microscopic nematodes.

A call to your local CTAHR office, describing your pest problems, may give you the exact solution. Your local nursery can also be of great help in solving your pest problems.

Below are descriptions of common pests you may encounter in your garden and ways to combat them. Many individual vegetable entries in this book also tell you how to combat pests attracted to that particular plant.

APHIDS

These pinhead-sized pests, often brown or white, are more easily controlled if found early, before they have taken over a plant. They suck the sap from your plants, causing the leaves to drop off. Aphid infestation can also spread viral diseases among your plants. Ladybugs are a natural control for aphids.

If ladybugs do not control your aphids, spray plants with an insecticidal soap, according to the package directions, or hose aphids off the plant with a strong blast of water. If the aphid infestation becomes severe, use Diazinon or Malathion, following package instructions carefully. Aphids are attracted to areas where ants are also present, so keeping ants and ant colonies out of your garden will help control your aphid population.

CHINESE ROSE BEETLES

Chinese rose beetles are dark brown, hard-crusted beetles about $1/2$ inch long. They attack beans, corn, and taro plants. These destructive beetles feed only at night and rest during the day just below the surface of the soil. You will know you have a problem with Chinese rose beetles when you notice that the leaves of your plants look like lace or have been totally stripped. Often, only the skeleton of the leaf remains.

Control Chinese rose beetles by handpicking them out of the soil during the day or handpicking them off the plants after dark (using a flashlight!). Or place a piece of paper or plastic below the plant and shake the plant to release the beetles. Destroy them by placing them in a bucket of soapy water. If infestation becomes a severe problem, control by using Diazinon or Sevin, carefully following package instructions. (Take care when using Sevin, as it can be deadly to the beneficial honeybee.)

CUTWORMS

Once you see the damage a cutworm can do to your vegetable plants you will know why it is called a cutworm. These large larvae of night-flying moths actually cut off young seedlings at the ground, leaving perhaps $1/4$ inch of stem protruding. It looks as if someone has intentionally gone to one of your healthy seedlings and cut it off with a knife or scissors, leaving the stem lying on the ground.

Cutworms feed at night, as well as on cloudy days. If you suspect cutworm damage, carefully scrape the dirt around the affected plant with your finger. You need only go down about $1/2$ inch to find the culprit, curled up in the ground. Cutworms will attack almost any young seedling, whether it be lettuce, parsley, corn, or broccoli.

If you have only a few seedlings to protect from cutworms, you can make a physical barrier by placing a cut-off paper cup or milk carton (quart size) over each seedling, burying the cup or carton in the ground about 2 inches and leaving about 2 inches exposed aboveground. These collars can be removed once the stems of the plants are thick enough to deter the cutworm.

If you have too many seedlings to make this method of protection feasible, try handpicking the cutworms in the evening or on cloudy days. Destroy them by placing them in a bucket of plain or soapy water (we use old paint cans for a bucket). If you know you have a cutworm problem, spray the top of the soil, just AFTER planting your seeds, with Sevin, Diazinon, or something called BT (bacillus thuringiensis). BT, which is a bacteria that controls cutworms, can be used on all crops up to harvest. Look for it under different trade names.

FRUIT FLIES (FLESH-EATING)

There are basically four different fruit flies you may find attacking your garden area: the melon fly, often found in the lower elevations of our state; the medfly, or Mediterranean fruit fly, found in the upper elevations; the oriental fruit fly, found just about anywhere; and the solanaceous fruit fly, found at all elevations that average less than 100 inches of rain per year. They all have large, distinctively patterned wings, and a wingspan from $1/4$ to $1/2$ inch.

Fruit flies lay their eggs on the flesh of fruits and vegetables. The eggs hatch into maggots, which feed on the flesh. These maggots, wiggling white larvae, cause the fruits and vegetables to be soft and mushy, and are easy to see in the infested flesh.

The different varieties of fruit flies can be major pests to beans, cucumbers, eggplant, squash, tomatoes, and, especially, sweet peppers. They attack both the fruits and stems of these plants, in the latter case preventing the actual formation of the fruit.

Fruit fly damage can be controlled in several ways. Pick susceptible vegetables when only $1/4$ ripe. Remove any fruit that has fallen to the ground to prevent attracting fruit flies and further infestation. Bury any infested fruit at least 3 feet deep, to prevent the larvae from surviving and multiplying. Put a netting tent over zucchini. Or, if you want to take the time, place small paper bags over the individual tomato, cucumber, or squash fruits. And, finally, check your local nursery for fly bait and traps. The combination of luring, baiting, and then trapping the flies has proven very effective, and environmentally safe, for the home gardener.

If fruit fly infestation becomes a major problem, contact the CTAHR for the current recommended insecticide treatment.

MITES

Mites, or spider mites, look like tiny spiders, and are usually red. If the leaves of plants are yellowed and curled, they may be infested with mites. You might also see fine webs under the affected leaves. To combat mites, spray the leaves with water. Continue to keep the leaves clean, since dust attracts mites. (You may notice more mites during periods of drought because of their attraction to dust.) If infestation becomes a problem, try spraying the plant with an insecticidal soap or light-grade horticultural oil.

NEMATODES

The root knot nematode is a microscopic roundworm that lives in the soil. It attacks the roots of many vegetables, including lettuce, tomatoes, peppers, corn, cabbage, and carrots.

Indications of nematode infestation are poor growth, lack of vigor, and wilting. Carrots will be stunted and deformed, with yellowed leaves. Taking a closer look, you will find that the roots of the affected plants have large lumps.

Root knot nematodes travel very slowly by themselves. However, they can be easily spread when you transplant infested plants to a new area. The best way to avoid nematode damage is to create an environment less hospitable to them by including a lot of organic matter in your garden soil.

Only one chemical soil treatment currently on the market kills nematodes. However, its purchase is not practical for the home gardener. It is expensive, since it is sold only in large quantities and the unused portion cannot be effectively stored for later use.

As an alternative, try to control nematodes by interplanting with marigolds or asparagus, both of which repel nematodes. Don't contaminate uninfected areas by transplanting plants from known infected areas. Wash your tools before using them in different garden sections. You can also alleviate the problem by rotating susceptible crops.

If you have the time and room, you can "solarize" the soil: during the warmest time of the year (if possible), remove all crop and weed residues from the soil in one section of your garden. Smooth and level the soil; water. Spread a thin, clear piece of plastic over the prepared area. Bury all edges of the plastic, sealing the covered area. Keep covered for 1 to 2 months. Remove the plastic and prepare soil for planting again.

The use of green manure in your garden will also deter or destroy nematodes. Try growing a green manure crop of C. Tropic Sun Crotalaria, working the plants into the soil when they mature. And finally, planting nematode-infested areas of your garden with mustard greens seems to eliminate the pests for several years. Plant the Florida broadleaf variety. When the plants are mature, till the plants into the soil. Remember to harvest some of the leaves for eating, if desired.

If nematodes continue to be a problem, consider planting your nematode-susceptible vegetables in containers, rather than directly in your garden plot.

SLUGS

The slug, which is a snail without its shell, can be a constant problem in the garden. Working at night, the slug feeds on the tender leaves of many varieties of plants. First you might notice a small curved bite out of a leaf. Next you might notice that the entire leaf is gone. Another indication that you have slugs is a shiny trail curving through the garden plot.

Slug pellets and bait, bought at your local markets, are effective, but are very dangerous to dogs and young children. Therefore, if you use them, be sure to read label instructions and precautions carefully. Additionally, sprinkle the pellets out sparingly, rather than making piles. Piles of pellet poison can be very inviting to dogs, who may think that dry dog food has been left out for them.

Better yet, instead of chemicals, use a beer trap, described on page 11, to attract and destroy slugs. Or place a piece of board or plywood in the garden, elevating it about $^1/_2$ inch off the ground. This attracts slugs away from your garden plants. You can then scrape the slugs into a bucket of plain or soapy water. If you squash a slug on the underside of the board before placing it in the garden, the slugs will be more attracted to the trap. A third way to deter slugs is to spread a thick layer of wood ash on the surface of the soil around each plant or around your garden's perimeter. Slugs will not crawl over the wood ash.

WHITE CABBAGE MOTHS

You will know that white moths are a problem in your garden if 1) you see them flying around and 2) your cabbage plants, including broccoli, have large holes and notches eaten out of the leaves. Control white moths by spraying plants with insecticidal soap. If infestation becomes a major problem, dust with Sevin or garden dust, according to package directions, or try BT, found in your local garden shop.

WHITEFLIES

The whitefly is a rather new pest to our islands, but the many varieties being introduced to Hawai'i wreak havoc among vegetable growers here.

Most of the damage caused by the whitefly is seen on vegetable plants such as breadfruit, eggplant, and pepper. The immature whitefly, called a crawler, looks like a tiny barnacle and attaches itself to plants as a barnacle would to a rock. The crawler then literally sucks the juices out of the leaf or plant it has attached itself to, weakening and ultimately killing the plant.

The crawler quickly develops into an adult, which is about $^1/_8$ inch long and looks somewhat like a tiny white moth. It also sucks the fluids from plants and rapidly reproduces and lays eggs on more plants. Again, these eggs quickly hatch into the devastating crawlers.

The best way to control whitefly infestation is with insecticidal soap, which destroys the crawlers but does not harm natural predators, like ladybugs, as much as pesticides do. Spraying the affected tree or plant with a strong spray of water can also be effective. Keeping your plants as healthy and vigorous as possible enables them to more easily combat the effects of whitefly infestation.

The following vegetables are arranged in alphabetical order for easy reference. As appropriate for each plant, descriptions include information on requirements, selection, preparation, planting, watering, weeding, fertilizing, pruning, harvesting—and eating, including recipes.

ALOE

No, aloe is not edible, but it does belong in every cook's garden. The aloe is a succulent grown widely in Hawai'i, and for good reason. The juice from the aloe leaves is used as an ointment to treat burns. Simply break off a small piece of an aloe leaf and gently rub the sappy juice from the leaf directly onto the burn. It may smell awful, but works as well or better than what you have in your medicine cabinet.

REQUIREMENTS: Since the aloe is a cactuslike plant, it requires sun and very little water. Plant your aloe near the kitchen door, if possible, since so many burns originate in the kitchen. If you live in an area with heavy rainfall, you can still grow aloe by planting it in a container, away from moisture, perhaps on your lanai.

SELECTION: Aloe self-multiplies, so try to obtain a small start from a neighbor's plant. Simply dig along the edge of the mature plant and pull apart a leaf clump that also contains a few roots. Or buy a small plant from your local nursery.

PREPARATION: A mature aloe plant can grow to a foot or more in diameter, with thick leaves 9 inches to 12 inches long. When selecting a place for your aloe, consider its size at maturity, since your plant will be a permanent fixture in your garden for years to come.

Aloe will grow in just about any well-drained soil. If the area where you are going to plant the aloe does not have good drainage, work in some coarse sand or pea gravel.

PLANTING: Plant your aloe very shallowly, just covering the roots and lower tip of the plant.

WATERING AND FERTILIZING: Watering is usually not necessary—water once a month at the most. Applying a small amount of manure tea (see page 2) once a year will keep your plant healthy for years.

The artichoke is a perennial grown for its edible flower—a delicious vegetable still being "discovered."

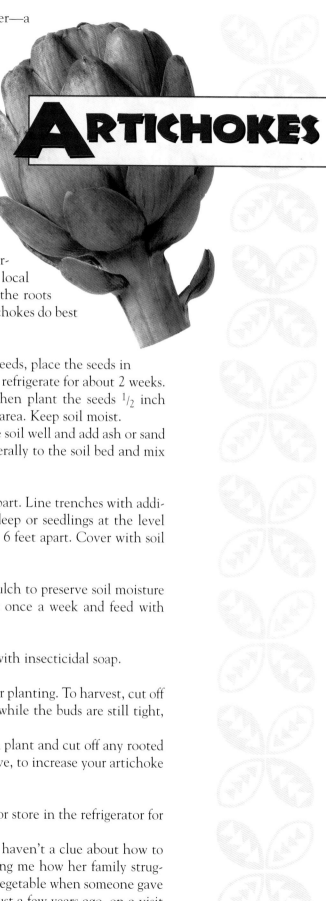

ARTICHOKES

REQUIREMENTS: The artichoke plant can be grown in most areas of Hawai'i, but prefers a cooler, foggy climate. For better success with growing artichokes in your area check with your local nursery, as there are some varieties of artichokes that are adapted to warmer climates. It requires space, full sun, good drainage, and abundant moisture. If you are planting in the warmer coastal areas of Hawai'i, select an area of your garden or yard that provides afternoon shade.

SELECTION: Artichoke seeds are available at most garden shops, or look for dormant root divisions at your local nursery, usually during January and February. Planting the roots tends to be more successful for the home gardener. Artichokes do best in Hawai'i if planted in the early spring.

PREPARATION: If you are going to start plants from seeds, place the seeds in a self-sealing plastic bag filled with moist peat moss and refrigerate for about 2 weeks. This helps the otherwise stubborn seeds germinate. Then plant the seeds $1/2$ inch deep in seed pots or directly into your prepared garden area. Keep soil moist.

To prepare your garden area for artichokes, work the soil well and add ash or sand if your soil is heavy. Add compost and aged manure liberally to the soil bed and mix in well.

PLANTING: Form trenches 6 inches deep and 7 feet apart. Line trenches with additional compost or aged manure. Plant roots 4 inches deep or seedlings at the level they were in their pot. The plants should be about 4 to 6 feet apart. Cover with soil and water deeply.

WATERING AND FERTILIZING: As plants grow, mulch to preserve soil moisture and to keep weeds under control. Water deeply about once a week and feed with manure tea once a month.

PEST CONTROL: If aphids become a problem, spray with insecticidal soap.

HARVESTING: Artichokes mature about 100 days after planting. To harvest, cut off the buds (the "artichoke"), along with 1 inch of stem, while the buds are still tight, plump and unopened.

About once every 3 years, carefully dig around each plant and cut off any rooted suckers from the main plant. Plant these suckers, as above, to increase your artichoke crop.

EATING: For best flavor, cook and serve immediately, or store in the refrigerator for up to 1 month.

I have been surprised at the number of people who haven't a clue about how to cook—or eat—artichokes. I remember my mother telling me how her family struggled to try to figure out how to prepare the odd-shaped vegetable when someone gave them several artichokes during the Depression. Then, just a few years ago, on a visit to a mainland grocery store, I took advantage of a sale on artichokes and bought several. A young girl come up to me and said her mother wanted to know how to cook artichokes. I gladly shared my limited knowledge for the preparation of my favorite vegetable. This simple recipe below is for those of you who have wanted to prepare artichokes but didn't know how.

STEAMED ARTICHOKES

Cut the stem off of each artichoke, level, to a length of about $^1/_2$ inch. Place stem-side down in a large pan containing about 1 inch of water. Cover and bring to a boil. Simmer for about 40 minutes, until you can easily pierce the side of the stem with a fork. Remove and serve immediately, or serve cold with a vinaigrette dressing.

To eat, pull off individual leaves; dip thick leaf end in butter, lemon-butter, or mayonnaise, if desired. Then, holding pointed end of leaf, slide leaf through your teeth to remove the tender pulp from the other end of the leaf. When all leaves have been eaten, you will come to the "heart" and "choke" of the bud. The heart is the tender portion of the bud attached to the stem, and the choke is the clump of fine, hairlike leaves covering the heart. Carefully remove the choke from the heart by scraping it off with a dinner knife. Dip heart lightly in butter or mayonnaise and enjoy!

STUFFED ARTICHOKES
Serves 6

6 large artichokes
4 cups cold water
$^1/_2$ cup lemon juice
2 slices white bread
$^1/_4$ cup water
2 anchovy fillets, finely chopped
$^1/_4$ cup plain dry breadcrumbs

3 tablespoons finely chopped garlic
3 tablespoons fresh parsley, chopped
2 tablespoons capers, chopped
$^1/_2$ teaspoon salt
$^1/_4$ teaspoon ground pepper
4 tablespoons vegetable or olive oil

Cut a little off the bottom of each artichoke stem to make it flat and even.
Snip off the sharp tips of each leaf with a scissors.
Cut off the topmost part of each artichoke with a very sharp knife.
Open each artichoke slightly by spreading the leaves apart, so you can get to the choke. Cut around the choke with a sharp, pointed knife.
Scrape the choke out of each artichoke with a small spoon.
Place prepared artichokes in a large bowl containing the cold water and lemon juice. This prevents the artichokes from turning brown while you are preparing the stuffing.
Remove and discard the crusts from the bread; sprinkle the bread with the $^1/_4$ cup water and let sit for 5 minutes. Squeeze out water and place bread in a bowl.
Add remaining ingredients, except oil, and mix well.
Drain artichokes well. Fill cavities and some spaces between leaves with stuffing.
Place artichokes in a large baking pan, stem-side down.
Sprinkle artichokes with oil.
Add water to the baking pan to a depth of about $^1/_2$ inch.
Cover the baking pan tightly with foil.
Bake at 375 degrees for about 1 hour, or until artichoke stems are tender at the base of the artichoke.
Serve immediately.

18

An annual, leafy salad vegetable, arugula (also called roquette) has grown in popularity in recent years because of its spicy, nutty flavor. Many restaurants, as well as "salad mixes" found in your grocery store, now use the distinctive arugula leaf to add zest to green salads. You can also use the flower of the plant as either a garnish or a part of your salad.

ARUGULA

REQUIREMENTS: Arugula is easy to grow and is ready for harvest in 6 to 8 weeks, but it needs cool weather. You will probably grow it successfully only in the cooler, higher elevations of Hawai'i like Kula, Maui, and Waimea on the Big Island. Avoid planting during the warmer months of the year.

SELECTION: Seeds are available at most local nurseries.

PREPARATION: Prepare soil by working in compost or manure. Thoroughly mix in $1/2$ cup of 10-30-10 fertilizer for every 10 square feet of garden space.

PLANTING: Plant seeds $1/4$ inch deep and 4 to 6 inches apart. Rows should be about 10 inches apart. Cover seeds with soil and tamp down lightly. Water gently but well. Or plant in a seedbed and transplant seedlings as you would for Mānoa lettuce.

WATERING AND WEEDING: Keep plants weed-free and water to keep soil slightly moist during entire growing cycle. Mulching the bed helps keep weeds under control and retain needed moisture.

HARVESTING: Harvest the entire plant and use leaves in salads or soups. Or cut just the outside leaves from the plant when they are no more than 6 inches long, leaving the remainder of the plant to produce additional leaves. Be sure the leaves are no longer than 6 inches; otherwise they will be too mature and will have a harsh flavor and odor.

EATING: Serve in salads, sandwiches, or soups for a spicy flavor variation.

GARLIC LINGUINE WITH ARUGULA

Serves 2 to 3

4 ounces linguine
2 teaspoons olive oil
1/4 cup red or yellow bell pepper,
julienne cut
1 tablespoon thinly sliced garlic
1/4 teaspoon salt
1/8 teaspoon crushed red pepper flakes
1 cup tightly packed chopped arugula
Grated Parmesan cheese (optional)

Cook linguine according to package directions, being sure to omit the salt; drain
well, reserving 1/4 cup liquid.
Heat oil in skillet over low heat; add bell pepper, garlic, salt, and pepper flakes.
Sauté over low heat for 5 minutes, stirring occasionally so garlic does not burn.
Place arugula in large serving bowl.
Add reserved cooking liquid, linguine, and bell pepper mixture.
Toss well and serve with grated Parmesan cheese, if desired.

SCRAMBLED EGGS WITH ARUGULA

Serves 2

4 eggs
3 tablespoons light cream or milk
1 teaspoon fresh thyme leaves, minced
1/4 teaspoon salt
1/4 teaspoon ground pepper

6 asparagus spears, cut in 1-inch pieces
1/2 cup grated Gruyere cheese
1 tablespoon dried breadcrumbs
3 tablespoons butter or margarine
2 cups chopped arugula leaves

Beat eggs, cream, thyme, salt, and pepper together.
Simmer asparagus in boiling water in a covered saucepan until tender,
about 3 minutes. Drain and pat dry on paper towels.
Toss cheese and breadcrumbs with asparagus until well combined.
Meanwhile, preheat broiler.
Melt butter in large fry pan over medium heat.
Add arugula and sauté until barely wilted, about 1 minute.
Add egg mixture; reduce heat to low, and cook about 3 to 4 minutes, until bottom of
eggs is set but top is still liquid.
Sprinkle asparagus mixture on top of eggs.
Place fry pan under broiler for 2 to 3 minutes, until top of eggs is golden brown.
Serve hot.

An area in your garden for asparagus is well worth the space, time, and effort. If you have never had fresh-picked asparagus, you are in for a tasty surprise. When we harvested our first spears, there weren't enough for a meal, so I went to the local market and bought more asparagus to combine with ours. What a shock! The asparagus from the market, although "fresh," didn't come close to tasting like our sweet, tender spears. It was like comparing fresh to canned. Find out for yourself!

ASPARAGUS

REQUIREMENTS: Asparagus needs a dry season to thrive, so you may have trouble growing this wonderful vegetable if you live in an area of our islands that is almost constantly wet. Asparagus should grow just about anywhere else in Hawai'i, however. Asparagus prefers full sun, although partial shade is acceptable. Asparagus also performs better in areas where there are cooler evenings.

SELECTION: Unless you have nothing else to do but baby-sit seedlings, save yourself a lot of time and disappointment by buying year-old asparagus crowns from your local nursery, rather than growing your asparagus from seed. Crowns are usually available from January to March, so plan to do your planting then.

PREPARATION: When deciding where to put your asparagus crop, remember that you will be planting in a bed that will last 10 to 20 YEARS. Consider putting your asparagus bed in your front yard, since the plants are fernlike and will make a beautiful, delicate addition to your landscaping.

With a place for a permanent bed in mind, the most important thing you can do to ensure a successful crop, year after year, is to prepare your bed well. This is the only chance you will get, so do it right the first time.

You want your soil to be light, rock- and root-free, and well drained. Till under the soil with plenty of compost or aged manure. A soil pH of 5.5 to 7.0 is ideal.

Bed preparation is crucial: dig a trench 12 inches wide and 16 inches deep. Trenches should be 3 to 4 feet apart. Refill the trench with about 10 inches of soil that has been mixed with compost or well-rotted manure. Tamp down the soil.

PLANTING: Place the crowns in the trench, $1^1/_2$ feet apart, with their roots spread out. Cover with 2 inches of soil. Water. As the shoots begin to grow, fill in the trench with additional soil, almost entirely covering the shoots. Continue this process until the trench is finally filled and the shoots protrude from the soil about 2 inches.

WATERING AND WEEDING: Water deeply on a regular basis. Weed the bed carefully, by pulling if possible, so you do not damage the asparagus roots. Mulching your asparagus bed with dry leaves, hay, grass clippings, or other mulching material helps control weeds and also improves the soil.

FERTILIZING: After the first year your crowns are in the soil, the fernlike stalks will turn brown and die back. Remove and destroy the stalks after they die back to prevent the spread of any diseases that may be present. Fertilize with manure tea (see page 2).

HARVESTING: When your asparagus bed is a year old, you will notice young spears beginning to poke out of the ground. This first year, harvest only $1/3$ of the spears. Let the remaining spears mature into fern stalks. In succeeding years, you can pick all spears for about 4 to 6 weeks; then let all the spears mature into fern stalks.

To harvest, cut off the spear with a sharp knife, carefully and at ground level, when the spear is about 8 inches long and the tips are tight and compact. Be sure to harvest all spears before they get taller than 8 inches. Otherwise, the plant will have difficulty sending up new spears. Stop harvesting spears before they reach $1/2$ inch in diameter.

If your asparagus bed is healthy and thriving, you can force two harvests per year: one in February to March, and one in August to September. To do this, simply stop watering your bed for 1 month, in July. This will force your fern spears to dry and die back. Cut off the dead spears, fertilize with manure tea, and begin watering again. Your asparagus should be ready to harvest again in a few weeks. If your bed seems to be struggling, forego the August harvest. Simply fertilize, continue to water on a regular basis, and harvest only during the February to March period.

Over the years, simply do the following to maintain your asparagus bed: fertilize every January and July with manure tea, water on a regular basis, and mulch to keep weeds in check.

EATING: Steam asparagus until crisp-tender; serve with lemon butter or mayonnaise, if desired. Add cooked, chilled asparagus to green salads.

ASPARAGUS WITH SHIITAKE MUSHROOMS
Serves 3 to 4

$1/2$ pound fresh asparagus (about 18 to 24 spears)
$1/2$ pound fresh shiitake mushrooms
$1/4$ cup butter
$1/2$ cup shallots, minced

2 tablespoons fresh gingerroot, minced
$1/2$ teaspoon salt
$1/4$ teaspoon ground pepper
$1/4$ cup dry vermouth

Cut asparagus into 1-inch pieces and mushrooms into $1/4$-inch strips. Set aside.
Sauté shallots and ginger in butter for about 3 minutes, until lightly browned.
Add asparagus, mushrooms, salt, and pepper. Sauté 2 minutes.
Pour vermouth over vegetables; cover pan and simmer 3 minutes.
Serve immediately.

NORWEGIAN-STYLE ASPARAGUS
Serves 3 to 4

24 asparagus spears (about $1/2$ pound)
$1/3$ cup butter
1 large, hard-boiled egg

Break asparagus into serving-sized pieces.
Steam until crisp-tender, about 3 minutes.
Meanwhile, allow butter to soften to room temperature.
Mash egg with a fork. Mix in softened butter.
Serve over hot asparagus.

Often thought of as only an ornamental, bamboo is an ideal plant for the home vegetable garden here in Hawai'i. The contrast between the delightful taste of fresh bamboo shoots and that of the canned variety is similar to the contrast between fresh garden peas and canned peas. Many Asian restaurants here in Hawai'i now refuse to use anything but fresh bamboo shoots in their dishes. Bamboo is easy to grow, and with plants becoming more readily available for purchase, there is no reason why edible bamboo should not be a part of every vegetable garden in Hawai'i.

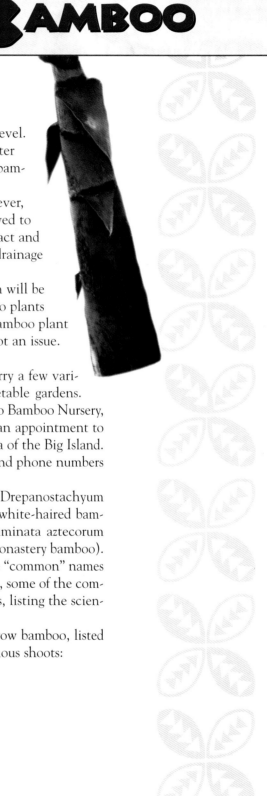

BAMBOO

REQUIREMENTS: Bamboo will grow anywhere in our islands (depending on the species), even as high as 3,500 feet above sea level. It prefers full sun, but tolerates partial shade, especially in the hotter areas of Hawai'i. The basic requirements for successfully growing bamboo are sun, warmth, nutrients, and moisture.

A pH of 5.5 to 6.5 and a well-drained soil are preferred. However, bamboo can do well in very wet areas as long as water is not allowed to stand, particularly when the plants are young. If your soil is compact and has poor drainage, plant your bamboo on a hillside to solve your drainage problem.

The edible bamboos you will be planting in your home garden will be the noninvasive, clumping varieties. This means that your bamboo plants will not send out the rambling, uncontrollable runners that the bamboo plant is so famous for. Thus, containment of the plant and its roots is not an issue.

SELECTION: Some select nurseries throughout the state now carry a few varieties of edible bamboo that are quite suitable for backyard vegetable gardens. However, an excellent Hawai'i mail-order source is the Quindembo Bamboo Nursery, located on the Big Island. Call Quindembo Bamboo Nursery for an appointment to visit their wonderful nursery next time you are in the Waimea area of the Big Island. You can then select your desired plants first-hand. Their address and phone numbers are listed under Suppliers in the back of this book.

Five excellent varieties for your home garden are the Drepanostachyum Khasianum (Himalayan bamboo); the Gigantochloa albociliata (white-haired bamboo); the Nastus elatus (New Guinea bamboo); the Otatea acuminata aztecorum (Mexican weeping bamboo); and the Thyrstostachys siamensis (Monastery bamboo). I apologize for using mostly scientific names. However, most of the "common" names for various bamboos are still in languages other than English! Also, some of the common names currently used are not widely known in all areas. Thus, listing the scientific names will help ensure that you get the right plant.

For those fortunate enough to have large areas in which to grow bamboo, listed below are several varieties of larger bamboo plants that bear delicious shoots:

Bambusa amhemica (digeridoo bamboo)
Bambusa burmanica (Thaikawa)
Baumusa edulis
Dendrocalamus membranaceous (Thai bamboo)
Gigantochlua atter (Indonesian sweet shoot bamboo)
Dendrocalamus asper (Phai Tong Koo)
Dendrocalamus brandesii (Velvet leaf bamboo)
Dendrocalamus giganteus (Dragon bamboo)
Dendrocalamus Latiflorus (Chinese sweet shoot bamboo)

You will be delighted with the taste of these varieties, but the plants will command a larger area of your yard than the smaller varieties.

PREPARATION: Prepare the soil by mixing in well-rotted manure. You can also add a general 8-8-8 fertilizer if your soil lacks nutrients, since a rich soil will result in better shoot production.

PLANTING: You may choose to locate your bamboo plant in your yard, using it as an edible landscaping plant, or consider planting the bamboo along one edge of your vegetable garden, allowing the beautiful plant to double as a windbreak.

For each bamboo plant, dig a hole twice as large as the existing container and then refill one-third of the hole with prepared soil. Remove the bamboo plants from their nursery containers, taking care to disturb the roots as little as possible. Place the plant in the hole so that when the hole is filled the soil level at the trunk of the bamboo is the same as it was in its original container. Be sure to firm soil well around the plant. Water deeply.

Let your bamboo plants grow, without harvesting, for the first 2 years after planting, especially if you are starting with the smaller, 1-gallon plants. You can then harvest a small amount of shoots the third year.

About a month before the first summer of growth, and then all years thereafter, watch for the small shoots to appear around the base of the mother plant. Begin mounding around the base of your bamboo plant with mulch, dry leaves, or straw, keeping the new shoots nearly covered. This mounding is not only beneficial to the growth of the plant and the flavor of the shoots, but it also makes it easier to harvest the shoots a few weeks later. Do this mounding of shoots whether you will be harvesting or not.

WATERING: Water your bamboo plants deeply when the soil becomes dry.

HARVESTING: Bamboo shoots are ready to harvest when they are about 2 inches in diameter at the base and 1 to 2 feet tall. Harvest time will be between May and October.

To harvest, pull the mulch away from the base of the plant, exposing the young shoots. Break the plant off at the bottom of each shoot where the base goes from wide to narrow. To keep your plants producing vigorously throughout the years, do not harvest more than $1/3$ of the shoots per year. That way, each year you will have a larger and larger harvest of these delicious vegetables.

After harvesting the shoot, peel the tough outside culm leaves, exposing the tender heart of the bamboo shoot. The discarded leaves make wonderful additions to your compost pile.

EATING: Slice the bamboo shoot heart into chunks 2 to 4 inches long, then quarter lengthwise. Soak in cold water about 12 hours, discarding and replacing the water several times. Then, cover the shoots with water and boil for 20 to 30 minutes, depending on the variety of bamboo shoot and your personal taste. Discard the water and repeat the boiling once more, adding 2 teaspoons salt to the water. Some people actually eat the Mexican weeping bamboo raw. With a little bit of experimentation you will come up with the process that will suit your tastes best. Freshly cooked bamboo shoots may be served alone, with butter and salt to taste. Or use in any recipe calling for canned bamboo shoots.

Cooked bamboo shoots store well in the refrigerator for several days or can be frozen in self-sealing plastic bags or other freezer containers for later use.

RICE SALAD
Serves 4 to 6

2 cups water
$1/2$ teaspoon salt
$2/3$ cup rice, uncooked
$1/4$ cup dried shiitake mushrooms, chopped
1 cup canned bean sprouts
1 medium Japanese cucumber
1 cup fresh boiled bamboo shoots, cut into $1/4$-inch strips
$1/2$ cup cooked ham, cut julienne style
5 tablespoons salad oil
5 tablespoons lemon juice
3 tablespoons rice wine (sake)
2 tablespoons shoyu
$1/8$ teaspoon salt

Bring water and salt to a boil. Add rice; cover and cook for 15 minutes.
Place hot rice in a colander; pour cold water over rice; drain well.
Soak mushrooms for 20 minutes in enough hot water to cover; drain well.
Drain bean sprouts.
Cut cucumber in half, then into thin slices lengthwise, then into 2-inch-long strips.
Place rice, mushrooms, bean sprouts, bamboo shoots, ham,
and cucumber in a large bowl.
Combine oil, lemon juice, rice wine, shoyu, and 1/8 teaspoon salt. Mix well.
Pour over rice mixture and toss thoroughly.
Cover and chill in refrigerator for about 1 hour.
Serve on lettuce leaves.

SHRIMP AND BAMBOO SHOOTS
Serves 3 to 4

2 cups water
2 tablespoons mirin
3 tablespoons shoyu
$3/4$ pound shrimp, shelled and deveined
1 pound fresh bamboo shoots, previously boiled

Combine water, mirin, and shoyu; bring to a boil.
Add shrimp and cook just until done, about 4 to 6 minutes.
Slice bamboo shoots into small pieces; add to shrimp and steam for 2 minutes.
Drain and serve with rice.

BEANS

Beans, both the bush and the pole varieties, are easy to grow and are rich in vitamins A, B1, B8, and C. The University of Hawai'i has developed several disease- and pest-resistant seed varieties that are suited for Hawai'i's gardens.

REQUIREMENTS: Beans should do well anywhere in Hawai'i. Bean seeds are sensitive to excessive moisture, so if you live in one of the wetter areas of our state, plant your beans during the drier months. A well-drained soil will also help prevent the bean seeds from rotting.

Beans prefer a well-drained soil with a pH of 6.0 to 7.5. Since beans are susceptible to diseases, it is recommended that you rotate your crop every year. Also, space your plants far enough apart to allow for good air flow, and do not touch or harvest bean plants when the leaves are wet.

SELECTION: Pole beans require added support, but produce up to 3 times as many beans as the bush variety. Excellent varieties that do well here in Hawai'i are the Poamoho pole bean, which is nematode resistant as well as stringless, and the Hawaiian Wonder pole bean, which is also nematode resistant.

Bush beans grow low to the ground and do not require support unless subjected to wind. If you want to grow bush beans try Greencrop, which does well in Hawai'i and is resistant to rust (reddish brown spots on leaves, stems, and pods).

Lima bean plants will last for a year if kept disease free. Some lima bean varieties that do well in Hawai'i are King of the Garden and Florida Butter (pole beans) or Fordhook 242, Allgreen, and Thorogreen (bush beans).

Bean seeds are readily available from the Department of Horticulture of the University of Hawai'i (see **page xx**), seed racks at local supermarkets, and local nurseries.

PREPARATION: Prepare the soil by adding 1 cup of 10-20-20 fertilizer per 50 square feet of garden area and work in well.

PLANTING: Plant pole beans along a fence or trellis in a single row, 1 inch deep and about 6 inches apart. Or make poles from freshly cut saplings or bamboo. Place poles about 2 feet apart in rows 3 feet apart. If desired, angle 3 or 4 poles together, teepee fashion, for stability. Plant 6 bean seeds around each pole. Cover seeds with soil and tamp lightly. Water. When seedlings are about 2 inches tall, thin and keep the best 3 or 4 plants in each group.

Plant bush bean seeds 1 inch deep about 3 inches apart in rows about 2 feet apart. Cover seeds with soil and tamp down lightly. Water.

WATERING AND FERTILIZING: Pole beans germinate in about 14 days, bush beans in about 7 days. Keep soil slightly moist until germination; then water deeply at least once a week if it doesn't rain. Water low, keeping water off leaves, and do not allow the soil to dry out. Apply mulch around plants to conserve moisture and keep the soil cool during the hotter days. Otherwise, hot spells can cause the plants to drop their blossoms, drastically reducing your harvest.

When plants are about 4 weeks old, side-dress with 10-20-20 fertilizer, about 1 tablespoon per plant. Or fertilize with manure tea. Be sure the fertilizer does not touch the leaves or stems of the bean plant.

PEST CONTROL: If cutworms are a problem, spray soil at time of planting with Diazinon and continue to spray weekly, according to package directions. Diazinon also effectively controls French bean fly infestation, which is indicated by the wilting and dying of the top of the bean plant when it is 2 to 4 weeks old. Discontinue use of Diazinon as beans begin to appear on the plants. Malathion may be used up to 1 day before harvest. USE EXTREME CARE WHEN USING PESTICIDES AND READ AND FOLLOW PACKAGE INSTRUCTIONS AND WARNINGS CAREFULLY.

HARVESTING: Green beans (pole and bush) are ready for harvest about 6 weeks after planting—about 10 days after the plant blooms. Harvest just before the seeds inside the pod begin to swell or before they become visible as bumps on the outside of the pod.

Lima beans are cultivated in the same way as green beans. However, harvest lima beans when the beans inside the pods are full-sized, but before the pods begin to turn yellow.

Old bean plants are high in nitrogen and a beneficial addition to your compost, so dispose of them by adding them to your pile.

EATING: Slice into bite-sized pieces and steam until crisp-tender. Stir-fry with other vegetables or add to soups and stews.

BEANS WITH MISO
Serves 4 to 6

1 pound fresh green beans, cut into 1-inch pieces
3 tablespoons toasted sesame seeds
2 tablespoons miso
2 tablespoons sugar
1/3 cup mayonnaise

Steam beans in a small amount of water about 15 minutes, until tender (or microwave, covered, for about 4 minutes).
Mix remaining ingredients together; combine with beans. Serve hot or cold.

GREEN BEANS WITH MACADAMIA NUT–LEMON BUTTER
Serves 4

1 pound fresh green beans, cut
1/4 cup butter or margarine
1/2 cup toasted macadamia nuts, chopped
1 tablespoon lemon juice
1 teaspoon fresh parsley, minced
1 1/2 teaspoons fresh basil, chopped
1/2 teaspoon salt

Steam beans in covered saucepan about 15 minutes, until crisp-tender.
Meanwhile, melt butter in small saucepan until it begins to brown.
Add nuts, lemon juice, parsley, basil, and salt. Heat 1 minute.
Drain beans; add butter-nut mixture and toss to coat. Serve immediately.

BEETS

If you are looking for a tasty vegetable that is easy to grow anywhere in Hawai'i, beets are the crop for you. Both the traditional beet root AND the leafy green tops are edible, the greens prepared and eaten in the same manner as spinach.

REQUIREMENTS: Beets prefer sun, but can be grown in semishade. A loose, well-drained soil, free of roots and rocks, is preferred, but beets will also grow in heavier soils. Add compost to the heavier soils to lighten them. Beets may be planted and harvested all year long. However, if you are in an area that has hot summers and falls, sow seeds to harvest in your cooler months and soak the seeds in water overnight to aid germination. If space in your garden is a problem, consider growing beets in a container.

PLANTING: Plant beet seeds $^1/_2$ to 1 inch deep, spacing them about 4 inches apart. Rows should be about 1 foot apart. Water lightly. Keep soil moist. Germination will occur in 10 to 20 days.

Beet seeds are actually a cluster of seeds, so you will probably get 2 or 3 seedlings for each seed you plant. When seedlings are about 4 inches high, thin to 1 plant in each cluster; transplant the thinnings or serve the tender leaves in a fresh salad—or cook as you would spinach. Tamp down the soil around the remaining seedling.

WATERING AND FERTILIZING: Beets must have consistent moisture and be weed-free. To ensure rapid growth, feed your beet plants every other week with manure tea (see page 2). If you have a problem growing beets, you are either not watering your plants consistently enough, or your soil pH is too acid. To correct the soil and bring it up to a pH of 6.0 to 7.0, add about 1 pound of dolomite limestone to 25 square feet of garden space and work into the soil prior to your next planting.

HARVESTING: Beets mature in 60 to 80 days. Any time prior to harvesting the root, you can pick up to $^1/_3$ of the plant's leaves for table use.

The top of the beet root will usually become visible near harvest time. Roots have the highest quality when they are 2 to 3 inches in diameter. You can leave them in the ground for up to a month or more after maturity, harvesting as needed, but some quality may be lost.

To harvest, carefully pull the beets out of the soil. Dust off soil and twist off the green tops, about 1 inch from the root, to avoid bleeding from the beet root. Prepare beets, and leaves, as soon as possible, or store beet roots in a cool place until ready to use.

EATING: Steam roots until tender; then slice and serve warm or chilled. Prepare beet greens (the leafy tops) in the same manner you would spinach.

STEAMED BEETS

Wash beets under cool water to remove any remaining soil. Place beets in a saucepan containing about 1 inch of water; cover pan with lid. Bring to a boil; reduce heat and simmer for about 45 minutes, until beets are pierced easily with a fork. (Check pan occasionally to be sure water remains in pan; add water if necessary.) Remove beets from pan when done. Cut off stem; carefully peel the thin skin from the beets with a paring knife. Slice beets $^1/_4$ inch thick and serve, warm or cold, with a small amount of butter or mayonnaise, if desired. Or cool and slice julienne style and serve in a green salad.

CITRUS BEETS
Serves 4 to 6

8 beets, each about 2 inches in diameter
$^1/_2$ cup sugar
$^1/_4$ cup red wine vinegar
$^1/_4$ cup orange juice
2 teaspoons cornstarch
$^1/_2$ teaspoon salt
$^1/_4$ teaspoon ground pepper
1 tablespoon butter or margarine
Grated zest of 2 oranges

In a medium saucepan, cover beets with water; bring to a boil. Cover; reduce heat, and simmer about 45 minutes, or until tender. Drain; rinse under cold water. When beets are cool to the touch, slip off the beet skins and cut beets into $^1/_2$-inch chunks.

Combine sugar, vinegar, orange juice, cornstarch, salt, and pepper in a saucepan. Bring to a boil over medium heat, stirring constantly, until mixture has thickened and is clear, about 5 minutes. Add butter and orange zest; stir until butter is melted; remove from heat.

Pour sauce over beets and serve.

BITTERMELON

Bittermelon is a relative of cucumber, squash, and watermelon and has similar growing habits. Known as balsam pear on the mainland, bittermelon looks like a wrinkled cucumber and has been a vegetable and medicinal favorite in the Philippines and other parts of Asia for centuries. Its juice, even today, is used in home medicine for tumors, diabetes, constipation, fever, colic, and many other maladies. Recently, the bittermelon juice has been used experimentally in an effort to inhibit HIV and AIDS.

As a vegetable, bittermelon is considered an acquired taste because of its bitterness. (Sorry, neither my family nor I like it at all.) However, harvested and eaten young and immature, the bittermelon can become a valuable and appreciated vegetable in Hawai'i's backyard gardens. It is easy to grow, as well as fast growing, and will thrive almost anywhere in our islands as long as it has warmth and water. The immature fruits are a good source of vitamin C and also contain some iron, phosphorus, and vitamin A. Usually considered an annual vine, bittermelon can be grown as a perennial here in Hawai'i as long as you harvest all the fruits before they ripen.

REQUIREMENTS: The bittermelon grows on a hearty vine that will need a trellis to contain it in your garden. The vines themselves resemble tomato vines. Pineapple field-workers used to plant bittermelon seeds in the pineapple fields, in the rows between the pineapple plants, where the vines were allowed to ramble. This practice made good use of the unused field space and provided a favorite vegetable on the dinner tables of pineapple field-workers.

SELECTION: Obtain bittermelon seeds from your local nursery, or use seeds gathered from a fully ripened fruit.

PREPARATION: Bittermelon prefers a well-drained soil over which has been scattered approximately $1/2$ cup of 10-30-10 fertilizer for every 4- x 6-foot garden plot. If your soil is heavy clay or lacks nutrients, mix compost and rotten manure into the soil prior to planting. Ideal pH for the soil is 5.5 to 6.5.

PLANTING: Seeds may be planted any time during the year in Hawai'i. Plant seeds $1/2$ inch deep, 18 to 24 inches apart, along a 6-foot-high trellis. Space rows 3 to 4 feet apart. Vines will emerge about 1 week after seeds are planted.

WATERING AND FERTILIZING: Water the seedbed deeply and irrigate deeply whenever soil becomes dry. Try to water the soil without wetting the leaves to prevent diseases.

The growing vines will benefit from the addition of 1 tablespoon of 10-30-10 fertilizer per vine every 6 to 8 weeks; or fertilize with manure tea.

PEST AND DISEASE CONTROL: Bittermelon are susceptible to pests and diseases, such as fruit flies and powdery mildew, common to other melon and squash crops. Pests may be controlled with a light application of a vegetable garden dust, Diazinon, Sevin, or Malathion. Powdery mildew, indicated by a white powdery substance on the leaves, may be controlled by spraying baking soda on the leaves once a week (mix 2 tablespoons baking soda in 1 cup water and pour into a spray bottle for easy application). Powdery mildew seems to be a greater problem for bittermelon vines that are grown in the cooler, moister areas of Hawai'i. USE EXTREME CARE WHEN USING PESTICIDES AND READ AND FOLLOW PACKAGE INSTRUCTIONS AND WARNINGS CAREFULLY.

HARVESTING: The first fruit will be ready to harvest about 90 days after planting. Harvest the fruit while it is still immature. The fruits should be firm, light green, oblong, pointed at the blossom end, and about 4 to 6 inches long. Keep a watchful eye on your bittermelon vines, because the fruit should be harvested about 8 to 10 days after it has flowered. Immature fruits are less bitter; the mature fruits are extremely bitter—even inedible, perhaps even toxic. You may, however, want to allow a few fruits to fully ripen so you can use the seeds from the ripened fruit for your next planting.

Store newly harvested bittermelon in a cool area for up to 2 weeks, but do not refrigerate.

EATING: Bittermelon is usually prepared by slicing it in half lengthwise and then removing and discarding the yellow or white seed core. It is then cut into slices about $1/2$ inch wide and either boiled, sautéed, deep-fried, or stir-fried. Sauté and add to omelets, or add to eggplant dishes. Or stuff with corned beef or pork hash mixed with chopped water chestnuts; steam until tender.

To remove some of the bitterness, roll pieces of bittermelon in salt, then gently squeeze out some of the juices. Or soak in salt water for 5 to 10 minutes. Another way to remove bitterness before using in recipes is to place sliced bittermelon in boiling water and boil for 3 minutes; drain; repeat if desired.

PORK AND BITTERMELON
Serves 6 to 8

1 pound pork, sliced into bite-sized pieces	$1/2$ pound shrimp, peeled and cleaned
3 tablespoons chopped garlic	4 medium bittermelon, chopped
1 small onion, sliced	$1/2$ teaspoon salt
1 cup diced tomatoes	1 tablespoon patis
	1 cup water

Sauté pork with garlic until slightly browned. Add onion, tomato, shrimp, melon, and salt. Sauté 2 minutes. Add patis and water; stir well.
Simmer, covered, 10 minutes. Serve immediately.

SCRAMBLED TOFU WITH BITTERMELON
Serves 4

2 medium bittermelon	1 6-ounce can corned beef
1 $1/2$ teaspoons salt	3 eggs, slightly beaten
$1/2$ block firm tofu, drained	Pepper to taste
4 tablespoons vegetable oil	

Cut bittermelon lengthwise into halves and remove seeds. Cut into thin $1/2$-inch slices. Sprinkle the slices with salt; rub salt into the bittermelon.
Let stand 15 minutes. Rinse bittermelon well under cold water;
drain well and blot dry with paper towels.
Break up tofu with fork and blot dry with paper towels.
Heat 2 tablespoons oil in fry pan; fry tofu until lightly browned. Remove tofu and set aside. Wipe pan clean and heat remaining 2 tablespoons oil; sauté bittermelon until tender. Mix in tofu, corned beef, and eggs.
Cover mixture, turn off heat, and let stand for 1 minute. Add pepper to taste.

BREADFRUIT

The breadfruit, or 'ulu, was a staple of the ancient Polynesians. It was introduced to our islands by the early Hawaiians and is referred to as a "Hawaiian Heritage Plant." It cannot be considered a "native" plant, since native plants are plants that were here before humans arrived. The "fruit" of the breadfruit tree is a high-carbohydrate vegetable that is a good source of calcium and vitamin B.

REQUIREMENTS: The breadfruit tree grows well in most areas of Hawai'i below 2,000 feet. The tree can grow 40 to 60 feet tall, with branches spanning from 30 to 60 feet. Although a beautiful shade tree, it may be unsuitable for the average home garden because of its size. However, if you have an area large enough to support such a tree, the breadfruit can be a rewarding addition to your yard.

PREPARATION: Select an area for your breadfruit tree that is sunny and warm and has well-drained soil and lots of room to grow. The tree has an extensive root system, so don't plant your tree to close to your other garden areas. Ideal soil pH range for breadfruit is 5.0 to 7.2.

Breadfruit trees prefer a rich, deep soil, so planting your young tree on top of an old compost pile is ideal.

SELECTION: Obtain seedling plants from your local nursery. Or propagate breadfruit from 9- to 10-inch-long shoots growing from the roots of a mature tree.

PLANTING: Place these cuttings in a shaded seedbed and cover with about $1/2$ inch of soil. Keep slightly moist. When a 2- to 3-foot top has grown, carefully transplant the young tree to a permanent area. You can start a plant from seeds, but the seeds should be no more than a month old. Seeds will germinate in 4 to 8 weeks. Be sure to transplant young trees grown from seeds to a permanent area when no more than 4 leaves have appeared, since more mature seedlings are difficult to transplant successfully.

Carefully plant your young tree with the top of the root line buried about 1 inch below the top of the soil, taking care to disturb the roots as little as possible. Water deeply and fertilize with manure tea or 10-20-20 commercial fertilizer.

WATERING AND FERTILIZING: Water the breadfruit tree frequently, since it does not tolerate drought. Even mature trees require occasional deep waterings in drier areas of Hawai'i.

Breadfruit trees begin to fruit in 3 to 6 years. The fruit grows to about 8 inches in diameter and weighs as much as 10 pounds. After the tree has finished bearing fruit each year, fertilize with about 2 cups of 10-20-20 fertilizer, working it deeply into the soil along the dripline of the tree's branches.

HARVESTING: Pick the breadfruit while it is still firm; it will soften in a few days. Take care when picking the fruit, since the branches are brittle and break easily. The breadfruit is ripe and ready to cook when the outside turns yellow or brown, rather than green. The breadfruit will be soft, and small sections of the rind will be flattened.

(Green breadfruit can also be eaten. The fruit will be hard when harvested. Very starchy, it is either baked or boiled until tender. Before peeling green breadfruit be sure to rub your hands with vegetable oil, to prevent staining from the white juices. Also, do not let any of the white juice get on clothing, because it will leave a permanent stain.)

EATING: To cook, remove the stem and the core of the breadfruit; quarter and remove rind. Sprinkle lightly with salt and garlic powder. Steam, in a covered pan, for 1 ½ hours. Or place prepared breadfruit in foil, wrap tightly, and bake for 1 hour. Serve with butter and sugar, if desired. Or slice steamed or baked breadfruit into ½-inch slices, fry in hot butter or oil until golden brown, and serve with butter.

BAKED BREADFRUIT
Serves 4 to 6

1 large, ripe breadfruit
1 cup water
³/₄ cup dark brown sugar
¹/₄ cup butter or margarine
¹/₄ cup lemon juice

Peel breadfruit. Place in a large saucepan with water; cover.
Bring to a boil; simmer for 1 hour.
Remove breadfruit from saucepan. Cut in half, remove core,
and slice breadfruit in 1-inch slices.
Butter a 9- x 13- x 2-inch pan; place half of the breadfruit in the pan. Sprinkle half of the sugar, butter, and lemon juice over the breadfruit; repeat with the remaining breadfruit slices, sugar, butter, and lemon juice, creating a second layer.
Bake at 350 degrees for 30 minutes. Serve immediately.

BREADFRUIT DONUTS

1 egg, beaten
1 cup ripe breadfruit, uncooked
2 tablespoons solid shortening
1 cup flour
¹/₂ cup sugar
3 teaspoons baking powder
¹/₄ teaspoon nutmeg
¹/₄ teaspoon cinnamon
¹/₄ teaspoon salt
Vegetable oil for deep frying
¹/₄ cup sugar
1 teaspoon cinnamon

Combine egg, breadfruit pulp, and shortening; mix well and set aside.
Sift next six ingredients together. Stir dry ingredients into breadfruit mixture.
Preheat oil to 370 degrees.
Drop donut mixture by teaspoonfuls into deep oil and fry until golden brown.
Remove and drain on paper towels.
Combine ¹/₄ cup sugar with 1 teaspoon cinnamon. Place in a brown paper bag.
Add warm donuts and shake to coat.
Makes 18 to 20 donuts.

Broccoli

High in vitamins A and C, calcium, and iron, broccoli is an ideal vegetable, whether eaten raw or cooked.

REQUIREMENTS: With a little care, broccoli will grow just about anywhere in Hawai'i, but grows better in the cooler areas of our state. When heads begin to develop, the broccoli needs cooler days and nights, so plant in the winter, October through March, if your area has warm, sunny summers. This will keep your plants from going to seed.

PREPARATION: Use a small spot in your garden as a seedbed for your broccoli, or plant seeds directly in the ground where you intend to have your mature plants. Your garden area for the mature broccoli plants should be well drained, and prepared about 2 weeks prior to planting either the seeds or seedlings, by tilling the soil well, adding compost and 10-30-10 fertilizer, and spraying the top of the bed with Sevin or Diazinon to control cutworms. Soil pH range for broccoli should be 6.0 to 7.5.

PLANTING: To plant in a seedbed and then transplant when young plants are 6 inches tall, prepare a small area about 1 x 2 feet by tilling soil with compost and a handful of 10-30-10, removing all weeds, and reducing soil to a fine, crumbly texture. Flatten the area and sprinkle lightly with broccoli seeds. Rub soil between your hands to sprinkle about $1/4$ inch of soil over the seeds. Tap soil lightly with the palm of your hand. Water lightly. Keep seedbed moist. Germination should occur in 5 to 10 days. When seedlings are 6 inches tall, gently plant in your prepared permanent bed, being careful to disturb the roots and soil around the roots as little as possible.

Plant the seedlings 18 inches apart, in rows about 2 feet apart. Be sure to plant the seedlings about 1 inch deeper than they grew in their seedbed, or almost up to the first leaf. This will produce a sturdier plant. Gently water your transplanted seedlings and continue to keep the area slightly moist.

To plant directly in the ground, prepare bed (see above). Plant 3 small broccoli seeds together, about 1 inch apart, in a triangle. Rub soil between your hands to sprinkle about $1/4$ inch of soil over the seeds. Tamp lightly with palm of hand. Plant each group of seeds about 18 inches apart, in rows about 2 inches apart. Gently water. Keep soil moist. When seedlings are about 6 inches tall, gently pull out the 2 smaller ones, leaving the largest seedling intact. Gently build up about 1 inch of soil around the stem of the remaining seedling and lightly tamp. Water gently and continue to keep the area slightly moist.

WATERING AND WEEDING: Broccoli plants need consistent moisture. If you are in an area with daytime temperatures above 75 degrees, mulch around each plant and between the rows with dry leaves, hay, grass clippings, or other mulch material.

Keep area weed-free by pulling out intruders; this will also help keep soil loose.

FERTILIZING: About 2 weeks after transplanting, pour manure tea (see page 2) around each plant, or carefully apply about 1 tablespoon 10-30-10 fertilizer around each plant and scratch into soil about 1 inch deep. Water deeply. Continue this fertilization every month until the main head is ready to harvest.

PEST CONTROL: You may wish to spray weekly with an insecticidal soap to control cabbage worms. Light applications of Sevin may be used for severe cases of infestation. USE EXTREME CARE WHEN USING PESTICIDES AND READ AND FOLLOW PACKAGE INSTRUCTIONS AND WARNINGS CAREFULLY.

HARVESTING: Depending on the variety, broccoli matures in 45 to 80 days. After you have harvested the large main head, smaller side-shoots will form and continue to appear for up to several weeks, extending your harvest up to 2 months. Be sure to rotate your crop after each harvest to prevent diseases.

Harvest your broccoli heads, and smaller side-shoots, just before the flowerettes begin to open and turn yellow.

EATING: Cabbage worms are almost impossible to avoid. So, to be on the safe side, soak your fresh broccoli in warm water to which you have added a little vinegar for about 15 minutes prior to serving raw or cooking.

Broccoli flowerettes may be eaten raw (perhaps with a dip), lightly steamed, or stir-fried.

Peel the stem of the broccoli, slice, and serve in stir-fried dishes, soups, or stews.

BEEF BROCCOLI
Serves 2 to 3

1 pound sirloin or flank steak	1 teaspoon sugar
1 $^1/_2$ teaspoons fresh gingerroot, grated	$^1/_2$ teaspoon salt
3 tablespoons shoyu	$^1/_4$ teaspoon pepper
3 tablespoons vegetable oil	1 tablespoon cornstarch
2 cups fresh broccoli, cut into bite-sized pieces	2 cups chicken broth
	4 green onions, cut into 1-inch pieces
1 medium round onion, sliced	

Cut steak into thin slices. Combine ginger and shoyu. Add meat and marinate for $^1/_2$ hour. Heat 1 tablespoon oil; sauté broccoli for 1 minute.
Remove broccoli from pan; heat other 2 tablespoons of oil; sauté meat and round onion until brown, about 4 minutes.
Combine sugar, salt, pepper, cornstarch, and broth. Stir into meat mixture. Add reserved broccoli and green onions; cook, stirring constantly, until sauce thickens. Serve with rice.

FRESH BROCCOLI SALAD
Serves 4 to 6

8 slices bacon
1 cup mayonnaise
$^1/_4$ cup sugar
$^1/_4$ cup red wine vinegar
3 cups broccoli flowerettes, chopped
1 medium onion, chopped
1 cup grated sharp Cheddar cheese

Fry bacon until crisp; drain and crumble. Combine mayonnaise, sugar, and vinegar. Mix with bacon, broccoli, onion, and cheese. Chill 1 hour.

BRUSSELS SPROUTS

Fresh Brussels sprouts are much more mild-tasting and sweet than those you buy frozen from the grocery store. Unfortunately, they are not suitable for growing in most areas of Hawai'i. They also take almost 4 months to mature. However, if your area meets the requirements below, you may want to try growing these tasty mini-cabbages.

REQUIREMENTS: If you live in an area where your daytime temperatures average 65 degrees or below for at least 3 months, you may be able to grow Brussels sprouts. You can find instructions for growing Brussels sprouts on the back of the seed packet and in numerous other gardening books.

Be aware that Brussels sprouts are susceptible to cabbage diseases, cutworms, and insect pests common to the cabbage family. Try to plant the Brussels sprout seeds in a garden area not previously used for cabbage, cauliflower, or broccoli.

PLANTING: Plant in a rich, well-drained soil. When you notice that sprouts are beginning to grow where the leaves join the stems, break off any lower leaves.

FERTILIZING: Fertilize each plant with manure tea or 1 tablespoon 10-30-10 fertilizer per plant when plants are about 8 inches high, and every 2 weeks thereafter.

HARVESTING: Harvest the Brussels sprouts when they are still compact and about 1 inch in diameter. Use a sharp knife to cut off each sprout, leaving enough of the trunk remaining so new sprouts can develop.

EATING: Use immediately for best flavor, or refrigerate until ready to prepare.

Soak Brussels sprouts in cold salted water for about 15 minutes prior to cooking to release any bugs that may be clinging to the vegetable. Before cooking, cut an X in the stem of each sprout so the stem will cook at the same rate as the head. Boil, steam, or braise.

BRUSSELS SPROUTS DELUXE
Serves 8

8 cups Brussels sprouts	1/3 cup dry breadcrumbs
1/2 teaspoon salt	1 hard-cooked egg yolk, mashed
1/3 cup butter or margarine	1 tablespoon chopped fresh parsley

Cut any large Brussels sprouts in half. Cook sprouts in boiling water for about 15 minutes, just until they are tender. Drain. Sprinkle with salt.
Melt butter in a saucepan; heat until butter just begins to turn brown; add breadcrumbs, egg yolk, and parsley. Mix well.
Pour sauce over Brussels sprouts; toss to cover. Serve immediately.

STEAMED BRUSSELS SPROUTS
Serves 4 to 6

3 tablespoons butter, melted	1/2 teaspoon salt
1 pound Brussels sprouts	1/2 teaspoon caraway seeds

Mix all ingredients in a microwave-safe bowl. Cover and cook on High for approximately 7 minutes, until sprouts are tender when tested with a fork.

Head cabbage is hardy and easy to grow. It stores well, is high in vitamins C and E and beta carotene, and is a good source of fiber—an ideal vegetable to include in your everyday diet.

REQUIREMENTS: Cabbage is a cool-weather crop, but if you plant it to grow and mature in Hawai'i's cooler winter months, you should be successful in cultivating this versatile vegetable. You can also try planting your cabbage next to a taller vegetable to allow the cabbage some afternoon shade.

CABBAGE

SELECTION: Plant varieties labeled Early for the best success. Savoy King is a heat-resistant variety.

PREPARATION: Cabbage prefers a soil with a pH of 6.0 to 7.0. Rotate cabbage crops every year, avoiding planting in an area that contained cabbage or any relative of cabbage in the last 3 years.

If cutworms are a problem in your garden, treat soil prior to planting seeds.

Prepare soil by working in about 1 cup of 10-30-10 fertilizer for every 3 x 10 feet of garden bed. Plant seeds $1/4$ inch deep in groups of 3 or 4 seeds. Space the seed groups about 1 foot apart in rows about 2 feet apart. Cover seeds with soil and tamp lightly. Water carefully. When seedlings are about 1 inch tall, cut off the less hardy ones.

WATERING AND WEEDING: Keep soil slightly moist at all times, watering as often as every day. Lack of water causes splitting of cabbage heads. Water plants below the leaves to avoid wetting the foliage, which could cause disease. Try using the flood-irrigation method: Wrap an old rag over the outlet of your garden hose. Turn on the water to a trickle and place the hose outlet next to the cabbage plant. Water will soak into the soil without water pressure from your garden hose digging holes in the ground.

Weed around your cabbage plants by hand-pulling, since cabbage has very shallow roots. Mulching the plants helps retain moisture and keep weeds in check.

FERTILIZING: Fertilize each plant every 4 weeks with about 1 tablespoon of 10-30-10 fertilizer or $1/2$ cup of manure tea.

PEST CONTROL: Spray with insecticidal soap, garden dust, or Sevin, according to package directions, if cabbage worms become a problem. USE EXTREME CARE WHEN USING PESTICIDES AND READ AND FOLLOW PACKAGE INSTRUCTIONS AND WARNINGS CAREFULLY.

HARVESTING: Cabbage matures in about 3 $1/2$ to 4 months. Pick cabbage when the heads are firm by cutting the cabbage off with a sharp knife. If you leave the stalks and roots in the ground, small cabbages may form, extending your original cabbage crop. Your harvested cabbage heads will keep well in the refrigerator for several months. If any of the heads split while growing, make those heads into sauerkraut.

EATING: A simple and delicious way to serve cabbage is to slice the raw cabbage very finely with a knife. Then, for every $1/2$-cup serving, chop 1 green onion and add to the chopped cabbage. Serve topped with 1 to 2 tablespoons mayonnaise.

FANCY COLESLAW
Serves 4 to 6

4 cups finely shredded cabbage
1 cup grated carrots
1 cup grated apples
1 cup mayonnaise
3 tablespoons vinegar
1 tablespoon honey
$^1/_4$ cup chopped red onion
$^1/_4$ cup raisins
1 teaspoon toasted sesame seeds
$^1/_2$ teaspoon salt
$^1/_4$ teaspoon ground pepper

Combine all ingredients, mixing well.
Chill, covered, several hours before serving.

SESAME SEED CABBAGE
Serves 4 to 6

1 head cabbage
1 tablespoon sesame seeds, toasted
1 tablespoon shoyu
1 teaspoon sugar
$^1/_4$ teaspoon pepper

Shred cabbage. Place in large pan with about $^1/_2$ cup water.
Cover and cook until cabbage is just tender.
Drain well.
Mix sesame seeds, shoyu, sugar, and pepper together.
Toss with cabbage and serve.

Carrots are ideal for the Hawai'i home vegetable garden, since they are easy to grow, are high in vitamins A and E and calcium, and may be grown and harvested all year long.

REQUIREMENTS: A root crop, carrots grow well in warm, arid climates, as well as in cooler, wetter areas of the state. If you do not want to dedicate a space in your garden to carrots, remember that they do well when grown in containers.

    If you live in a warmer climate and find that your carrots produce mostly greenery and little or no carrot root, try planting and harvesting carrots in the cooler months. Also consider allowing your carrots to grow and mature in the ground for 3 to 4 months, since carrot roots take longer to mature in warmer climates. Remember, too, that excess nitrogen will produce green tops on plants and inhibit the production of the root. Using a fertilizer with a lower nitrogen content may help solve this problem.

SELECTION: Several seed varieties are available at local garden stores. Which variety to buy depends mostly on personal preference.

PREPARATION: Thoroughly prepare the planting area prior to sowing the carrot seeds. Remove all rocks, and dig soil to a depth of 9 to 12 inches. Add compost to the soil, but be sure not to use fresh manure. The nitrogen in the fresh manure will cause many rootlets to form on the carrot, as well as produce a poor-tasting vegetable. Too much nitrogen will also cause the overproduction of green tops. Carrots prefer a soil pH of 5.5 to 6.5.

PLANTING: Seed packets provide varying instructions for sowing seeds, some more labor-intensive than others. A simple way to sow carrot seeds is in rows, LIGHTLY sprinkling an area 3 inches wide for the length of the row desired (preferably at least 2 feet long). Space rows 6 inches apart. Lightly cover the seeds with fine soil (approximately $1/4$ inch) rubbed between your hands. (Note that $1/4$ inch is a very small amount of soil. Do not plant too deeply or the carrot seeds will not germinate.) Lightly pat the covered seeds with the palm of your hand and sprinkle gently with water. Water daily. Germination should occur in 10 to 21 days.

WATERING: Keep carrot seedlings watered so the soil remains slightly moist. Even though the top crust of the soil is dry, the soil below may be adequately moist.

PEST CONTROL: Little knots along the roots of the carrot indicate the presence of nematodes (see page 14). Nematodes stunt the growth of carrots, so avoid their infestation by rotating your crops and adding plenty of compost before planting. If nematodes become a major problem, treat soil prior to the next planting.

HARVESTING: As the seedlings grow to maturity (in approximately 2 months), harvest the carrots that are growing close to others. Such thinning will give you an immediate harvest for the table, as well as allow the remaining carrots to grow larger. Carrots that are crowded may be oddly shaped, but they will still taste good. If the crowns of any carrots become exposed, cover them with soil. Otherwise, the crowns will turn green and be bitter-tasting.

    TIP: Harvest only the carrots you need for the table. Leave the rest in the ground for later harvest. This way you will have a fresh supply of carrots for weeks, possibly even months. Start a new seedbed of carrots just before you begin to harvest your first carrot, to ensure a continuous supply all year long.

EATING: It is unnecessary to peel carrots before serving, unless you want to. Cut raw carrots into thin strips, chill, and eat alone or with your favorite dip; grate raw carrots into coleslaw or lettuce salads; or, for a simple, nourishing side dish, grate 2 cups raw carrots, add $^1/_2$ cup raisins, and then mix in 3 tablespoons mayonnaise, or to taste. For cooked carrots, slice and steam lightly until just tender; add butter to taste just before serving, if desired. Add sliced carrots or carrot chunks to your favorite soups or stews about $^1/_2$ hour before cooking is complete. Or, just a few minutes before serving, add thinly sliced carrots to your favorite stir-fry.

CARROT CAKE
Serves 10 to 12

CAKE:

4 large eggs
1 $^1/_2$ cups vegetable oil
1 cup sugar
1 cup firmly packed dark brown sugar
2 cups flour
1 tablespoon baking soda
2 teaspoons cinnamon
1 teaspoon salt
3 cups grated carrots
$^3/_4$ cup chopped walnuts

ICING:

$^1/_2$ cup butter, softened
1 8-ounce package cream cheese
1 teaspoon vanilla
3 $^3/_4$ cups powdered sugar, sifted
$^1/_4$ cup finely chopped walnuts
2 tablespoons firmly packed dark brown sugar

Beat together eggs, oil, and sugars until fluffy.
Sift together flour, baking soda, cinnamon, and salt. Gradually add dry ingredients to egg mixture, mixing well. Add carrots and walnuts; mix well.
Bake in 2 greased and floured 8-inch round pans at 350 degrees for about 45 minutes, until toothpick inserted in center comes out clean.
Remove from oven; cool for 10 minutes. Remove from pans and cool completely.
For icing, beat together butter and cream cheese until smooth. Mix in vanilla.
Beat in powdered sugar, a little at a time, until smooth and creamy.
When cakes are completely cool, spread icing over top of one cake.
Place other cake on top and spread icing over top and sides.
Mix $^1/_4$ cup walnuts with the 2 tablespoons brown sugar.
Sprinkle nut mixture over top of cake. Chill until ready to serve.

VEGETARIAN "MEAT" LOAF
Serves 4 to 6

$^1/_4$ cup butter or margarine
1 large onion, chopped
1 pound fresh mushrooms, chopped
2 tablespoons minced garlic
4 $^1/_2$ cups grated carrots
5 eggs, slightly beaten
1 cup fresh breadcrumbs, divided

1 cup grated sharp Cheddar cheese, divided
2 teaspoons fresh basil
2 teaspoons fresh thyme
$^1/_2$ teaspoon salt
$^1/_4$ teaspoon pepper
1 tablespoon butter or margarine

Sauté onion, mushrooms, and garlic in butter until onion is soft.
Add carrots, eggs, $^1/_2$ cup breadcrumbs, $^1/_2$ cup cheese,
and remaining ingredients to onion mixture.
Spread mixture in a buttered bread pan or oblong baking dish.
Sprinkle the remaining breadcrumbs and cheese on top.
Dot with a little butter and bake, covered, at 350 degrees for 40 minutes.
Uncover and continue baking until browned, about 5 minutes longer.

40

Cauliflower, a good source of vitamin C, is a popular vegetable eaten raw or cooked and is not difficult to grow under the right conditions.

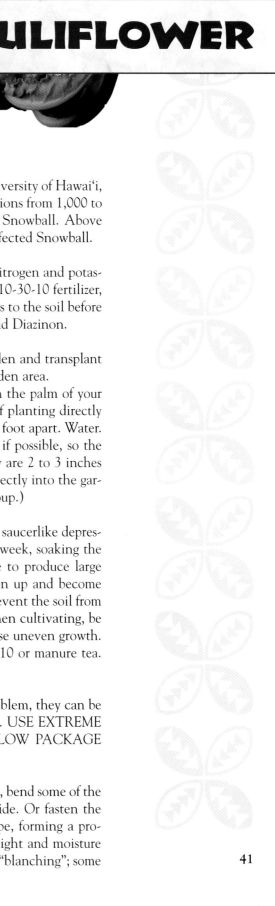

REQUIREMENTS: Cauliflower does not tolerate high temperatures. It will grow in the warmer regions of Hawai'i if you plant in October or November, so that the plants have warm weather in the early stages of growth and cooler weather as the head (curd) begins to form and develop. The developing cauliflower heads seem to love cold nights, so try to plan your planting schedule accordingly.

SELECTION: The Pua Kea cauliflower seed, developed by the University of Hawai'i, is especially suited for warmer climates below 1,000 feet. For elevations from 1,000 to 2,500 feet, try the Snow King, Snow Queen, or the Extra Early Snowball. Above 2,500 feet, try the Super Snowball, the Early Snowball, or the Perfected Snowball.

PREPARATION: Cauliflower needs a well-drained soil, rich in nitrogen and potassium, with a pH of 6.0 to 7.0. Prepare soil by adding compost and 10-30-10 fertilizer, working in well. If cutworms are a problem, apply Diazinon granules to the soil before planting and work it into the soil 3 to 6 inches, or spray with liquid Diazinon.

PLANTING: Start the cauliflower seeds in a seedbed in your garden and transplant 3 to 6 weeks later, or plant the seeds directly into the planned garden area.

Plant seeds 1/4 to 1/2 inch deep; cover with soil and tamp with the palm of your hand. If planting in a seedbed, place seeds about 3 inches apart. If planting directly into the ground, plant 2 to 3 seeds together, 2 feet apart, in rows 1 foot apart. Water. Seeds will germinate in 3 to 5 days. Water daily, in the morning if possible, so the plants will dry as soon as possible. Transplant seedlings when they are 2 to 3 inches tall and have the first pair of true leaves. (For seedlings planted directly into the garden, thin each set of seedlings to the sturdiest seedling in each group.)

WATERING AND FERTILIZING: As the plants mature, make a saucerlike depression around each plant to help hold water. Water at least once a week, soaking the soil to a depth of 6 inches. Cauliflower needs constant moisture to produce large heads; if the soil dries out between waterings, the heads will open up and become "ricey." Cultivate the soil frequently to keep weeds down and to prevent the soil from forming a crust; otherwise water will not be able to penetrate. When cultivating, be careful not to disturb the cauliflower roots, since doing so will cause uneven growth.

When plants are about 6 to 8 weeks old, fertilize with 10-30-10 or manure tea. Repeat again with manure tea just as heads begin to form.

PEST CONTROL: If pests (aphids, cabbage worms) become a problem, they can be controlled with vegetable garden dust, insecticidal soap, or Sevin. USE EXTREME CARE WHEN USING PESTICIDES AND READ AND FOLLOW PACKAGE INSTRUCTIONS AND WARNINGS CAREFULLY.

SPECIAL NOTE: When the cauliflower heads reach about egg size, bend some of the plants' leaves over the head and tuck them in on the opposite side. Or fasten the leaves at the top together with twine, rubber bands, or plastic tape, forming a protective "tent" over the cauliflower head. This tent will keep out light and moisture but still allow the heads to grow and air to circulate. (This is called "blanching"; some cauliflower varieties now are actually "self-blanching," with leaves that automatically fold over the young developing heads.) At this point, water only the roots of the plant, not the head or leaves. Gently unwrap the heads once in a while to check for pests or to let the heads dry out if it has rained.

HARVESTING: Harvest when the heads are compact and smooth and the buds are still tight and unopened. If the heads are irregular and uneven and have spaces, they were picked too late. To harvest, cut off just below the head, along with a few leaves. A morning harvest usually brings the best flavor.

EATING: To serve, cut cauliflower into individual "flowerettes." Serve raw with ranch dip, or place in a microwave-safe dish, cover with plastic wrap, and microwave on high for 4 minutes. Serve with salt and pepper. Or microwave for 3 minutes and top with $1/4$ cup of shredded cheddar cheese. Continue cooking, uncovered, for 1 more minute.

CAULIFLOWER CASSEROLE
Serves 6

1 $1/2$ cups milk
1 cup soft breadcrumbs
$1/4$ cup onion, finely chopped
1 tablespoon fresh parsley, chopped
1 teaspoon garlic salt
$1/4$ teaspoon paprika
$1/4$ teaspoon ground pepper
1 $1/2$ cups Cheddar cheese, grated
3 eggs, well beaten
1 $1/2$ cups fresh cauliflower, chopped in large pieces
(steamed, covered, in microwave for 5 minutes)

Heat milk; add breadcrumbs, onion, parsley, seasonings, and cheese. Stir well. Stir in eggs. Place cauliflower in a greased 1 $1/2$-quart casserole. Pour cheese mixture over cauliflower. Set in pan of hot water. Bake at 350 degrees for 1 hour.

CAULIFLOWER WITH NUTMEG SAUCE
Serves 4 to 6

1 head cauliflower
2 tablespoons butter
2 tablespoons flour
$1/4$ teaspoon salt
1 cup milk
$1/2$ teaspoon nutmeg

Cut cauliflower into flowerettes; steam in small amount of water until tender, about 10 minutes, or microwave (covered) for 4 minutes.
Melt butter in small saucepan over low heat. Stir in flour and salt. Add milk all at once. Cook over high heat, stirring constantly, until mixture thickens and bubbles. Remove from heat. Stir in nutmeg. Serve over cauliflower.

The two forms of Chinese cabbage are bok choy and won bok. The bok choy is more similar to Swiss chard than to a cabbage, since it does not form a head. Won bok has a long, compact head with crinkled leaves.

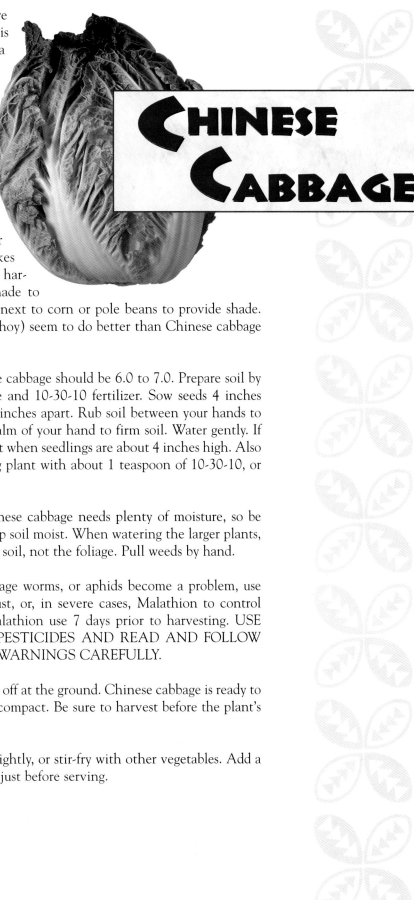

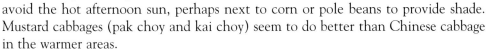

CHINESE CABBAGE

REQUIREMENTS: Since Chinese cabbage is a cool-weather crop, you may have difficulty growing it in the warmer areas of our state. However, you can experiment and try to overcome your hot-weather obstacle by planting in the winter months, since Chinese cabbage takes only about 9 weeks from planting to har- vest. Also, plant in partial or full shade to avoid the hot afternoon sun, perhaps next to corn or pole beans to provide shade. Mustard cabbages (pak choy and kai choy) seem to do better than Chinese cabbage in the warmer areas.

PREPARATION: Soil pH for Chinese cabbage should be 6.0 to 7.0. Prepare soil by working in compost or rotted manure and 10-30-10 fertilizer. Sow seeds 4 inches apart, $1/4$ inch deep, in rows about 12 inches apart. Rub soil between your hands to cover seeds and gently pat with the palm of your hand to firm soil. Water gently. If desired, thin plantings to 8 inches apart when seedlings are about 4 inches high. Also at this time, side-dress each remaining plant with about 1 teaspoon of 10-30-10, or with manure tea.

WATERING AND WEEDING: Chinese cabbage needs plenty of moisture, so be sure to water frequently enough to keep soil moist. When watering the larger plants, water just the bottom of the plant and soil, not the foliage. Pull weeds by hand.

PEST CONTROL: If cutworms, cabbage worms, or aphids become a problem, use insecticidal soap, vegetable garden dust, or, in severe cases, Malathion to control these pests, However, discontinue Malathion use 7 days prior to harvesting. USE EXTREME CARE WHEN USING PESTICIDES AND READ AND FOLLOW PACKAGE INSTRUCTIONS AND WARNINGS CAREFULLY.

HARVESTING: To harvest, cut heads off at the ground. Chinese cabbage is ready to harvest when the heads feel firm and compact. Be sure to harvest before the plant's seed stalk begins to form.

EATING: Serve raw in salads, steam lightly, or stir-fry with other vegetables. Add a few chopped leaves to soups or saimin just before serving.

CABBAGE BAKE
Serves 6

3 slices bacon, diced
$1/_2$ cup Portuguese sausage (mild), diced
1 Chinese cabbage, chopped into $1/_2$-inch-wide strips
1 cup diced onion
$2/_3$ cup chicken bouillon or chicken stock
2 cups cooked potatoes
2 egg yolks
2 tablespoons butter
$1/_2$ teaspoon salt
$1/_4$ teaspoon ground pepper
$1/_4$ cup milk (about)

Sauté bacon and sausage together until bacon is just crisp, about 4 minutes.
Add cabbage, onions, and bouillon.
Cover and steam about 10 minutes, until cabbage is tender and limp.
Pour into casserole dish.
Beat potatoes with egg yolk, butter, salt, pepper,
and enough milk to make potatoes smooth and creamy.
Spread mashed potatoes over cabbage mixture.
Place under broiler until potatoes are browned, about 3 to 4 minutes.

PORK AND CABBAGE
Serves 4 to 6

1 pound kālua pork (as found in 1-pound plastic tubs) OR 1 pound Chinese roast
pork, chopped
1 to 2 heads Chinese cabbage, chopped (about 12 cups)
1 medium onion, chopped
2 tablespoons fresh Chinese parsley (cilantro), chopped

Place pork in a large fry pan. Heat through. Add cabbage and onion. Stir well.
Reduce heat to low. Cover pan and simmer, stirring occasionally, until cabbage is
limp, about 15 minutes.
Sprinkle with cilantro and serve immediately.

Chinese peas are a delightful, slightly sweet vegetable high in thiamine, niacin, and riboflavin. Since Chinese peas are very expensive at your local market, they will make a valuable addition to your backyard garden.

REQUIREMENTS: Chinese peas will grow all year in Hawai'i, but prefer the cooler climates. If you live in the warmer, lower elevations, plant Chinese peas in October or November, to avoid the hot summer months. Also consider growing Chinese peas in the partial shade, or on your lanai in a container. High temperatures hasten the maturity of the Chinese pea plant, often making the plants short and stunted, and shorten the harvest time. During warmer weather the plants may also be less resistant to diseases.

SELECTION: Stick with the Mānoa Sugar variety of Chinese pea, available from the University of Hawai'i Department of Horticulture and some local markets and nurseries. This seed was developed by the Department of Horticulture specifically for Hawai'i growing conditions and is resistant to powdery mildew.

PREPARATION: Chinese peas are very susceptible to nematodes, so treatment of the soil prior to planting is important if nematodes are present. Chinese peas prefer a neutral soil of 7.0. Prepare soil by adding compost and 10-30-10 or 10-20-20 commercial fertilizer, working in well. Fertilize again 4 weeks after planting.

PLANTING: Plant seeds in a row, zig-zag fashion, 1 inch deep and 3 inches apart. Tamp soil lightly with the palm of your hand. Water. A dozen or so plants should serve your family well.

Construct a simple trellis, about 4 to 5 feet high, for the plants to climb on. You can simply place a few tree sticks in the ground along the pea line and run kite string between the poles, making horizontal rows with the string about 4 inches apart. Or use chicken wire supported by sticks. Use your imagination and whatever materials you have available.

WATERING: Water plants on a regular basis. Do not allow soil to dry out.

PEST CONTROL: Watch for cutworms, which love the young, tender Chinese pea seedlings. If cutworms are a problem, treat soil with Diazinon prior to planting, or spray when seedlings are about 1 inch tall.

HARVESTING: Harvest about 7 days after flowering and before the seeds start to swell. Daily harvesting may be necessary. If you want shelled peas, allow the pods to develop, then harvest when the peas inside the pod are the desired size.

EATING: Stir-fry or steam lightly until crisp-tender and serve. Do not overcook Chinese peas.

CHINESE PEAS WITH MUSHROOM SAUCE
Serves 4

1 cup sliced fresh mushrooms
1 can water chestnuts, sliced
1 cup chicken broth
1 tablespoon cornstarch
2 teaspoons shoyu
2 cups Chinese peas
1 cup green onion, cut in 1-inch pieces

Combine mushrooms, water chestnuts, and chicken broth in saucepan. Bring to
a boil; lower heat and simmer for 10 minutes, stirring occasionally.
Combine cornstarch and shoyu; add to mushroom sauce, along with Chinese
peas and green onions.
Cook, stirring constantly, for 3 to 5 minutes, until peas are crisp-tender.
Serve immediately.

SESAME PEAS
Serves 3 to 4

3 tablespoons sesame oil
2 cups Chinese peas
$^1/_2$ cup chopped green onion
2 tablespoons toasted sesame seeds
2 tablespoons pine nuts (optional)
$^1/_2$ teaspoon salt
$^1/_4$ teaspoon ground pepper

Sauté Chinese peas and onion in hot oil for approximately 3 minutes.
Stir in remaining ingredients. Sauté for 2 minutes. Serve immediately.

You don't need expansive Iowa fields to grow delicious corn on the cob. An area in your vegetable garden as small as 4 x 6 feet will do nicely. And once you have tasted corn fresh from your garden you will never buy another frozen ear of corn!

CORN

REQUIREMENTS: Our climate suits corn well. You should be able to grow corn anywhere in Hawai'i. However, if you live in a cooler, more rainy area, time the planting for July or early August, to allow for harvest in October, usually the warmest, driest month of the year. In the warmer, drier areas you should be able to plant corn almost year-round.

Corn takes considerable garden space and is a heavy feeder. If you do not plant a large enough section of corn, you will get poor pollination, resulting in a harvest of cobs with very few, or missing, kernels. Planting your corn in shorter rows (in a roughly square configuration), rather than in fewer, longer rows, promotes better pollination.

SELECTION: To ensure a more successful and more problem-free crop, plant only the University of Hawai'i variety of corn seeds. These seeds have been especially cultivated for Hawai'i's climate, diseases, and pests.

PREPARATION: Plan your area to allow space for at least 3 rows 2 to 3 feet apart. Again, short rows forming a square ensure better pollination. You can plant corn seeds twice as close together as recommended in gardening manuals as long as your soil is rich and fertile.

Prepare your garden area by working compost or rotted manure deep into the soil to promote drainage.

Dig trenches for each row about 5 inches deep and 3 inches wide. (By planting your corn seedlings in a trench, you create a firmer base for the corn stalk, making it less susceptible to wind damage.) Sprinkle each 6 feet of row with $1/4$ cup of 10-30-10 or 10-20-20 fertilizer. Cover with 1 inch of soil. Place 3 corn seeds in a triangle, 1 inch apart. Space these corn seed triangles 1 foot apart. Cover with 2 inches of soil. Tamp soil down lightly. Water trenches carefully. When you have completed planting your seeds, your trenches should still be about 2 inches below the original soil line. When seedlings are about 4 inches high, thin each triangle to the 1 healthiest seedling. Fill the trench in with about 1 inch of soil. When seedlings are about 8 inches tall, spread a band of 10-30-10 or 10-20-20 fertilizer, about $1/4$ cup per 6-foot row, along the trenches. Work fertilizer in lightly; then fill trench in with additional soil, making it level with the original soil line. Repeat fertilizing when plants are about 2 feet high, and mound soil about 3 to 4 inches over fertilizer and corn stalks, forming a long, aboveground mound in each row.

WATERING AND WEEDING: Water corn weekly, deeply along the trenches created by the mounding. Keep weed-free by carefully pulling the weeds by hand, to protect the shallow roots.

PEST CONTROL: If cutworms are a problem in your garden, treat the soil prior to planting, or handpick the worms until your seedlings are about 8 inches high.

HARVESTING: Corn is ready to harvest about 3 months after planting. It is ready to pick when the kernels at the tip of the cob are full and plump and the silks have browned and dried out. You will also notice that the ears will begin to lean away from the stalk when they are ready for harvest. Do not let the corn become overripe. If the kernels are a bit wrinkled, or are a deep yellow, the corn is overripe and starchy.

Pick the corn by carefully twisting the ear off the stalk. Pick just before you are ready to cook. Although newer varieties do keep longer after harvest, the sugar from the corn immediately begins to break down into starch as soon as the ear has been removed from the stalk. So, for best flavor and quality, eat immediately.

EATING: Overcooking corn can ruin it. For perfectly cooked corn on the cob, remove the husks and corn silks from the corn cobs. Bring a pot of water, sufficient to cover the corn, to a boil. Carefully drop the cobs into the boiling water. Cover pot and immediately set the timer for 6 minutes. At the end of the cooking time, remove the cobs from the boiling water and serve immediately, adding butter, salt, and pepper, if desired.

CORN PUDDING
Serves 4 to 6

2 cups milk
2 cups fresh-cut corn (3 to 4 ears)
3 eggs, slightly beaten
$1/4$ cup finely chopped onion
1 tablespoon butter or margarine, melted
1 teaspoon salt
1 teaspoon sugar

Scald milk. Combine milk with remaining ingredients and pour into a greased casserole dish. Set casserole dish in a shallow pan and place in a preheated 350-degree oven. Add about 1 inch of water to the pan.
Bake for about 45 minutes until pudding is done. To test for doneness, insert a knife into pudding, just off center. Knife should come out clean.
Remove from oven and let stand for 10 minutes.

GRILLED BBQ CORN
Serves 6

6 ears corn, in their husks
6 tablespoons butter, cut into 12 equal pieces

Soak the corn in a pot of cold salted water for about 1 hour.
(The wet husks steam the corn as it cooks, keeping it moist, and the salt water adds saltiness to the fresh corn.)
Carefully peel the husks back without detaching them at the bottom.
Remove the corn silk. Pull the husks back up around the corn, putting 2 pieces of butter in each ear. Be sure the husks completely cover the corn kernels.
Grill the corn over medium-hot coals, turning frequently, for about 20 minutes.
Salt and pepper to taste. Serve immediately.

The cucumber is an easy-to-grow vegetable high in vitamins A and C.

REQUIREMENTS: Well suited for Hawai'i's climate because they like warmth and humidity, cucumbers grow well in containers as well as in the ground.

SELECTION: Most popular here in the islands (and very expensive at supermarkets) is the Burpless Hybrid, or Japanese cucumber, which requires no peeling and has late-maturing seeds. (By the way, those variegated patterns on Japanese cucumbers you see on serving platters or in salads don't indicate a special variety; the cucumbers are just partially peeled prior to serving.)

PREPARATION: The soil in which you're going to plant cucumbers must be well drained. Work compost or well-rotted manure into the soil a week or two prior to planting. Cucumbers grow on climbing vines, so plant in an area where you can place a small "fence" or trellis next to your plants to provide support. The trellis should be at least 4 feet high.

HINT: In two areas of your garden, set up permanent trellises (one in each area) about 10 feet long. Rotate the planting of these areas between cucumbers and Chinese snow peas. (Plant cucumbers in area A and Chinese snow peas in area B; then, at the next planting, plant Chinese snow peas in area A and cucumbers in area B.) Rotating will help cucumbers avoid diseases, and the Chinese snow peas will help enrich the soil if you dig in the old plants after final harvest. Plant the cucumbers or Chinese snow peas on one side of the trellis and a low-bearing crop, like lettuce or carrots, on the other side of the trellis. This allows you to harvest your cucumbers or peas from both sides of the trellis, using both sides of the garden space without overcrowding trellis space.

PLANTING: Plant cucumber seeds in a row, zig-zag style, 6 inches apart, $1/2$ to 1 inch deep and about 1 to 4 feet from the trellis. Water lightly. When the seedlings are about 6 inches tall, carefully train them to climb on the trellis if they have not done so by themselves. Also at this time, before your daily watering, sprinkle about $1/4$ cup of 10-30-10 fertilizer per 1-foot row of plants, scratching soil lightly to work fertilizer in; or apply manure tea. Repeat every 2 to 3 weeks.

WATERING AND WEEDING: Cucumbers are mostly water, so consistent moisture is necessary for a successful crop. When the weather becomes very dry, water plants deeply. As the plant grows and matures, water low, avoiding the leaves. To deter the spread of diseases, water in the morning so leaves will have a chance to dry out during the day.

Carefully weed by hand.

PEST CONTROL: If the cucumber leaves are attacked by pests, spray lightly with vegetable dust or Sevin. Avoid spraying after fruits begin to appear.

HARVESTING: As fruits begin to appear, harvest as soon as they are ready, to allow the remaining cucumbers to properly mature. Do not allow the fruits to become too large or mature, or they may be dry and pulpy, and the seeds may be overly large. To ensure continuous production of new fruits, pick the cucumbers while they are very green, before the skin begins to yellow. If just one cucumber begin to turn yellow, the entire vine will stop producing and die.

To harvest, gently twist the cucumber, or snap at the stem, being careful not to disturb or injure the vine. The harvest period can last 4 to 6 weeks.

EATING: Serve raw, either alone or in salads. Pickle young cucumbers, or combine with a kim chee sauce.

CHILLED CHICKEN WITH CUCUMBERS

Serves 6 to 8

6 Japanese cucumbers
1 teaspoon salt
$^1/_2$ cup shoyu
$^1/_2$ cup sugar
$^1/_2$ cup cider vinegar
3 tablespoons sesame seeds, toasted
4 green onions, chopped
4 cloves garlic, minced
1 chili pepper, seeded and chopped
1 tablespoon dashi or chicken bouillon crystals
5 pounds chicken pieces, boiled, boned, shredded, and chilled.

Slice cucumbers into $^1/_4$-inch slices; salt and let stand 15 minutes.
Rinse under cold water and drain well. Chill.
Combine shoyu, sugar, vinegar, sesame seeds, green onions, garlic, chili pepper,
and dashi; mix well and chill.
Toss chicken and cucumbers with dressing and serve.

CUCUMBERS IN SOUR CREAM SAUCE

Serves 6 to 8

1 cup sour cream (regular or low fat)
2 tablespoons green onion, chopped
2 tablespoons vinegar
$^1/_3$ teaspoon prepared mustard
$^1/_4$ teaspoon sugar
$^1/_4$ teaspoon salt
$^1/_8$ teaspoon pepper
2 cucumbers, sliced thin

Mix all ingredients together. Chill and marinate 2 hours.
Serve as a side dish with ham, lamb, or beef.

DAIKON

Like the common radish, daikon (also called Chinese radish) is very easy to grow and is a rewarding addition to any backyard vegetable garden.

REQUIREMENTS: Daikon is a member of the turnip family. Because it is a root crop, daikon will grow well anywhere in Hawai'i as long as the soil is deep and well drained. For best results, avoid planting daikon during the hottest times of the year.

SELECTION: Seeds may be obtained from your local nursery.

PREPARATION: In preparing soil for planting, be sure to till deeply, at least 12 to 14 inches down, since the daikon root needs plenty of space to grow. Sprinkle the plot lightly with 10-20-20 commercial fertilizer and work in well.

PLANTING: Plant seeds $1/2$ inch deep and 4 inches apart, in rows about 10 inches apart. Cover with soil and water lightly.

WATERING: Water when top of soil becomes dry.

HARVESTING: Harvest the white daikon radish when the root begins to protrude from the ground. Cut off leafy tops about 1 inch above root. Store daikon in a cool, dry place, or refrigerate.

EATING: Some of the young daikon leaves may be harvested and steamed as a vegetable, added to soups, or made into tsukemono (ask your Japanese friends). Slice the white daikon radish into thin pieces and dip in shoyu. Cut in chunks and add to soups and stews or shoyu dishes a few minutes before serving. Or grate raw daikon and serve with sashimi.

JAPANESE PICKLES
Makes 1 dozen 8-oz. jars of pickles

6 cups thin-sliced daikon
3 cups thin-sliced cucumber (do not peel)
1 cup thin-sliced carrots
2 cups thin-sliced eggplant
$1/4$ cup salt
2 cups sugar
1 $1/2$ cups shoyu
3 tablespoons cider vinegar
1 Hawaiian chili pepper
$1/2$ inch fresh gingerroot, chopped fine

Mix daikon, cucumber, carrots, and eggplant with salt. Let soak overnight.
Drain liquid and squeeze vegetables to remove additional liquid.
Mix together sugar, shoyu, vinegar, chili pepper, and ginger in a saucepan.
Bring sauce to a boil. Add vegetables and mix well. Remove from heat.
Place vegetables and sauce in jars and refrigerate until well chilled.

ORIENTAL VEGETABLE SALAD
Serves 5 to 6

1 large daikon
1 large cucumber
2 carrots
$1/2$ teaspoon salt
$1/2$ pound fresh mushrooms
1 tablespoon chopped fresh dill
$3/4$ pound fresh shrimp, shelled and deveined
1 tangerine, peeled and broken into individual sections

DRESSING:

2 eggs
$1/4$ teaspoon salt
$1/4$ teaspoon sugar
3 tablespoons butter, melted
2 tablespoons red or white wine vinegar
1 teaspoon paprika

Grate daikon, unpeeled cucumber, and carrots into bowl; sprinkle with salt and toss
well. Let stand about 30 minutes; drain off any liquid.
Slice mushrooms thinly; mix mushrooms and dill with vegetables.
Sauté shrimp until just done, about 4 minutes; cool and add to vegetables.
Prepare dressing: Mix eggs, salt, sugar, and butter in top of double boiler.
Beat mixture over boiling water until smooth and creamy. Remove from heat and
gradually add vinegar, beating constantly until mixture cools; mix in paprika.
Pour dressing over vegetables and toss; top with tangerine sections and serve.

A source of vitamin C, phosphorous, and calcium, eggplant is a popular vegetable served in numerous ethnic recipes here in Hawai'i.

REQUIREMENTS: Eggplant does well in Hawai'i all year long, since it prefers warm weather and needs a long, warm growing period. You can avoid some eggplant diseases by rotating crops to a different area of your garden after each season. If space is a problem, consider growing eggplant in containers.

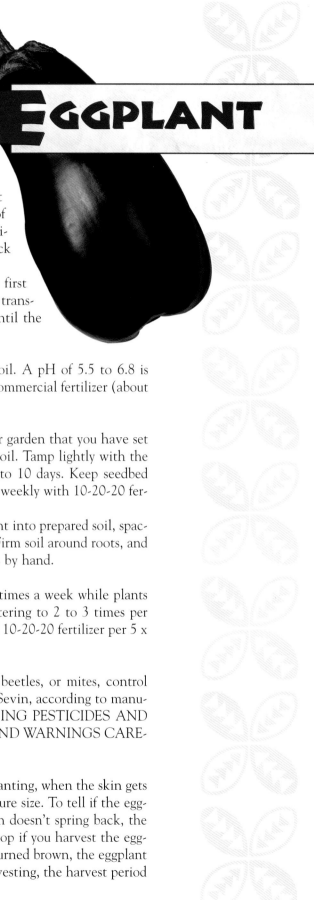

SELECTION: Seeds for the long variety of eggplant (Waimānalo Long) can be obtained from the University of Hawai'i Horticulture Department. Seeds for the round variety of eggplant (Florida Market, Burpee Hybrid or Black Beauty) can be found at your local market or nursery.

Hint: Since eggplant takes 4 to 6 months before the first harvest, interplant your lettuce seedlings with the eggplant transplants to take advantage of the empty spaces available until the eggplants grow larger.

PREPARATION: Eggplant prefers a rich, well-drained soil. A pH of 5.5 to 6.8 is ideal. To prepare the soil, work in compost and 10-20-20 commercial fertilizer (about 1 cup per 5 x 10 feet of garden space).

PLANTING: Sprinkle seeds lightly in a small area in your garden that you have set aside for seedbeds. Sow $^1/_4$ inch deep, covering with fine soil. Tamp lightly with the palm of your hand. Water. Seeds should germinate in 8 to 10 days. Keep seedbed moist. Two weeks after germination, fertilize the seedlings weekly with 10-20-20 fertilizer or manure tea.

When seedlings are about 4 to 6 inches high, transplant into prepared soil, spacing plants 2 to 3 feet apart, in rows about 2 $^1/_2$ feet apart. Firm soil around roots, and water transplants with 10-20-20 or manure tea. Pull weeds by hand.

WATERING AND FERTILIZING: Water deeply 1 to 2 times a week while plants are growing. As fruits begin to mature, increase deep watering to 2 to 3 times per week. Also at this time, carefully work in another 1 cup of 10-20-20 fertilizer per 5 x 10 feet of garden space.

PEST CONTROL: If you have infestation with aphids, beetles, or mites, control them with an insecticidal soap, garden dust, or a spray of Sevin, according to manufacturer's directions. USE EXTREME CARE WHEN USING PESTICIDES AND READ AND FOLLOW PACKAGE INSTRUCTIONS AND WARNINGS CAREFULLY.

HARVESTING: Harvest about 70 to 90 days after transplanting, when the skin gets a high gloss on it, or when the eggplant is $^1/_3$ to $^2/_3$ its mature size. To tell if the eggplant is ready to harvest, press the skin; if the indentation doesn't spring back, the fruit is ready to pick. You will harvest a more abundant crop if you harvest the eggplants before they reach full size. If the seeds inside have turned brown, the eggplant is too mature. With proper fertilization, watering, and harvesting, the harvest period will last 3 to 4 months.

EATING: Keep stem on eggplant until just before preparing. Eggplant does not store well, so plan to eat within 2 to 3 days after harvest.

Stir-fry, steam, or bake eggplant either alone or in your favorite recipe.

Chop eggplant into bite-sized chunks, steam, and serve warm or chilled with a mayonnaise/shoyu dip.

FRIED EGGPLANT WITH MISO
Serves 4

3 large eggplants

$1/4$ cup miso

2 tablespoons sugar

1 tablespoon mirin

3 tablespoons water

3 tablespoons sesame oil

2 teaspoons toasted sesame seeds

Slice eggplant into $3/4$-inch slices. Rinse under cold running water. Dry on paper towels. Meanwhile, mix miso, sugar, mirin, and water in small saucepan.

Heat, stirring constantly, until sauce becomes sticky.

Heat oil in skillet. Fry eggplant until tender.

Place fried eggplant on serving platter.

Pour miso sauce over eggplant; sprinkle with sesame seeds.

VEGETARIAN SPAGHETTI SAUCE
Serves 3 to 4

$1/4$ cup vegetable oil

1 pound eggplant, cut into $1/2$-inch cubes (about 2 cups)

1 medium onion, chopped

2 tablespoons minced garlic

1 tablespoon fresh parsley, chopped

1 28-ounce can Italian-style tomatoes

2 6-ounce cans tomato paste

$1/2$ cup dry red wine

1 4-ounce can sliced mushrooms

3 teaspoons dried oregano leaves

1 teaspoon salt

1 teaspoon sugar

Heat oil in large saucepan and sauté eggplant, onion, garlic, and parsley in oil until onion becomes tender. Stir in remaining ingredients, breaking up tomatoes into small pieces. Cover and gently simmer sauce for 1 hour, stirring occasionally.

Serve over cooked spaghetti and top with grated Parmesan cheese if desired.

REQUIREMENTS: Green onions can be planted all year long in Hawai'i. All you need is a well-drained, slightly acidic to neutral soil. Onions are affected by nematodes, so treat the soil prior to planting if nematodes are present. Green onions grow well in containers as well as in the ground, so consider placing a container for your green onions conveniently close to your kitchen door.

SELECTION: Only the multiplying (or dividing) type of green onion is grown successfully in Hawai'i and comes in two types: the small-leafed and the large-leafed (futo-negi) strains. Although chives are actually an herb, they are similar in appearance to green onions and can be grown in the same manner.

The green onion can be grown from "sets" obtained from your local nursery, as well as from seeds, available at most markets and from local nurseries. Follow package instructions for spacing and thinning. However, a highly economical and successful way to propagate the green onion is to plant the white ends of green onions you are using in your kitchen. Simply cut off about $1/2$ inch of the white end of the green onion, where the roots are still intact. (Note: This will not work if the market where you bought the green onions has cut off the root tips.) Let the onion ends dry overnight or for a day or two. Cut off any long roots, so the remaining roots are no longer than $1/8$ inch.

PREPARATION: Prepare a garden area for the green onions by adding compost and 10-30-10 fertilizer to the soil and working it in well. Place your prepared onion ends in the soil, the cut tops level with the soil, but not covered. Water lightly.

WATERING AND WEEDING: Water regularly to keep soil slightly moist. Keep area weeded.

HARVESTING: You can begin harvesting about 60 days after planting, but the onions can be left in the ground until needed. Harvest and use, however, before plants begin to flower.

To harvest, gently loosen soil around the green onion plant with a trowel and pull plant completely out. If you need green onion tops for your kitchen before your plants are mature, cut off the tops of several plants using a scissors. Leave about 2 inches of green top on each plant. Early harvesting of just the green tops, however, may prevent the white portion of the onion from growing as productively and may cause the overall plant to be smaller.

The green onions will keep better after harvesting if you do not cut off the ends with the roots (to replant) until you are ready to eat the onions.

EATING: Eat green onions raw, or lightly cook. Chives will lose their flavor if cooked, and should be used only raw. The green leaves of both chives and green onions may be chopped, placed in self-sealing plastic bags or old spice jars, and frozen for later use.

PEPPER STEAK
Serves 3 to 4

1 pound sirloin steak
$1/4$ cup shoyu
1 $1/2$ teaspoons fresh gingerroot, grated
2 tablespoons chopped garlic
1 tablespoon salad or vegetable oil
1 green pepper, sliced thin
2 stalks celery, sliced thin
1 tablespoon cornstarch
1 cup water
1 cup green onions, chopped
2 tomatoes, cut in 8 wedges each

Cut steak across grain into thin slices. Combine shoyu, ginger, and garlic; add
steak and marinate for $1/2$ hour. Heat oil in large frying pan.
Stir-fry steak; add green pepper and celery. Stir-fry about 5 minutes.
Mix cornstarch with water; add to fry pan along with green onions;
cook until thickened, about 2 minutes.
Add tomatoes and cook just until tomatoes are heated through, about 2 minutes.
Serve with rice.

BBQ SHRIMP SCAMPI
Serves 4 to 6

2 pounds shrimp (large)
$3/4$ stick butter, melted
$1/4$ cup olive or salad oil
2 tablespoons snipped fresh chives
1 tablespoon minced garlic
1 tablespoon minced shallots
$1/2$ teaspoon salt
$1/4$ teaspoon ground pepper
$1/4$ teaspoon paprika

Combine all ingredients except shrimp in bowl. Mix well.
Peel and clean shrimp.
Add shrimp to butter mixture; cover and refrigerate for 1 hour.
Grill over hot coals about 2 minutes per side. Serve immediately.
Barbeque marinated shrimp over hot coals until done, about 3 minutes per side.

An excellent source of fiber and potassium, lettuce is a favorite vegetable, and easy to grow. A pretty plant, lettuce works well as an edging for your flower garden. Lettuce also makes an ideal container plant.

LETTUCE

REQUIREMENTS: Although lettuce is a cool-weather crop, if you stick with the Mānoa (Green Mignonette) or Ānuenue lettuce varieties, you can grow lettuce anywhere in Hawai'i. However, in the warmer areas, plant lettuce in the cooler winter months. Otherwise, the hot sun will cause the tender lettuce plants to bolt before maturity. ("Bolting" occurs when the plant quickly goes to the flowering or seed stage, often making the edible portion of the plant tough and bitter.)

In the cooler, higher elevations, you can also successfully grow head lettuce. If you find you are having problems growing Mānoa lettuce in these cooler, wetter areas, try Ānuenue instead. Lettuce grows best in soil with a pH of 6.0 to 7.0, and it grows well in containers.

PLANTING: One method is to plant seeds directly into garden beds. Prepare the beds by working compost and $1/4$ cup 10-30-10 fertilizer per 25 square feet of garden space into the soil. Plant seeds $1/4$ inch deep in rows 1 foot apart and thin to 5 inches apart when seedlings are 1 inch tall. Thin to 8 to 10 inches apart when seedlings are 2 inches tall.

Another method is to plant in seedbeds for transplanting. You can plant your lettuce seeds in an area as small as 1 x 2 feet. Work soil well to remove all roots and stones. Level your seedbed area. Very lightly sprinkle seeds. Cover seeds with $1/4$ inch of soil by rubbing soil between the palms of your hands. Pat soil down lightly. Sprinkle area gently with water.

When seedlings are about 2 inches high, carefully dig up the largest seedlings and transplant them into a lettuce bed prepared by working compost and $1/4$ cup 10-30-10 fertilizer per 25 square feet of garden space into the soil. Make a small hole, about 2 inches deep, with your fingers and place the seedling in the hole, allowing the roots to fall freely into the hole. Cover the roots and $1/4$ inch of the seedling with soil, carefully pinching around the base of each seedling with your fingers to firm the soil. Space lettuce seedlings about 10 inches apart in rows 12 inches apart. Water transplanted seedlings gently but thoroughly. Keep area constantly moist, carefully watering at least twice a day, until seedlings take hold, about 4 days. Continue transplanting seedlings from the seedbed as they grow to about 2 inches tall.

If your vegetable garden has limited space, transplant lettuce seedlings in between rows of cabbage, cauliflower, or broccoli, or even into your flower garden. In warmer areas you can successfully plant lettuce in semishade.

WATERING AND WEEDING: Water lettuce plants to keep soil slightly moist. Do not let the lettuce wilt. Remember, lettuce is 95% water. To help retain moisture and to keep weeds under control, mulch with grass clippings or other similar mulching material.

FERTILIZING: When plants are about 3 inches in diameter, side-dress each plant with 1 tablespoon 10-30-10 fertilizer, working the fertilizer carefully into the soil. Be careful not to let the fertilizer touch the leaves, since it will cause them to brown and scar. Or fertilize with manure tea.

HARVESTING: Lettuce should be ready to harvest about 30 days after transplanting. To ensure a continuous crop of lettuce, plant new seeds in a seedbed just as you begin to transplant the previous seedlings.

EATING: Serve well-chilled as a salad or on sandwiches. Use as a garnish for fruit salads.

GREEN LEAFY SALAD
Serves 4 to 6

12 cups fresh lettuce, torn into bite-sized pieces
1 large clove garlic
3 tablespoons salad oil
1 tablespoon fresh basil, chopped
1 tablespoon fresh thyme, chopped
$1/2$ teaspoon salt
$1/2$ teaspoon ground pepper
4 tablespoons vinegar
1 cup thinly sliced tomatoes
$1/2$ cup grated carrots
1 cup salad croutons

Wash lettuce and pat dry; chill.
Cut garlic clove in half lengthwise and rub entire inside surface of large salad bowl, preferably wooden. Mince garlic and set aside.
Add chilled lettuce to bowl. Drizzle oil over lettuce; sprinkle with the minced garlic; toss until lettuce is coated and shiny.
Add basil, thyme, salt, and pepper, tossing well after each addition.
Add vinegar and toss well.
Add remaining ingredients; toss well and serve immediately.

HOT LETTUCE SALAD
Serves 2 to 4

2 cups torn lettuce leaves
1 cup torn fresh spinach leaves
$1/4$ cup diced celery
1 tablespoon chopped green onion
6 slices bacon
$1/4$ cup hot bacon drippings
1 tablespoon crumbled blue cheese
2 tablespoons sugar
$1/2$ teaspoon salt
$1/2$ teaspoon Worcestershire sauce

Combine lettuce, spinach, celery, and onion in large bowl.
Cook bacon until crisp, reserving $1/4$ cup bacon drippings; drain bacon on paper towels. Crumble bacon and add to greens.
Quickly combine remaining ingredients and pour over greens.
Toss lightly and serve immediately.

Onions are easy to grow and of course are indispensable in the kitchen. The island of Maui is famous for the sweet onion it grows.

ONIONS

REQUIREMENTS: Onions take about 3 months to mature, and that's if you start them from "sets" and not from seeds. If planting from seed, follow package directions; thin according to directions and use thinnings as "green onions."

Onion "sets," available from most local nurseries, are actually immature onion bulbs. Onions do best if the weather is cooler when the green tops are growing and warmer when the bulbs are forming, so plan to plant your onion sets to correspond to your particular weather. As a general rule, however, plant onions in December or January to harvest in the late spring.

SELECTION: Look for "short-day" varieties such as Yellow Granex hybrid, Early Texas Grano 502, Excel, Tropic Ace hybrid, or the Yellow Bermuda. An interesting note: the "Maui Onion," with its sweet, mild taste, is simply any one of the above varieties, but grown in the weather and soil conditions found in places such as Kula, Maui. If you prefer a stronger-tasting onion, try the 'Awahia, Red Creole, Early Harvest hybrid, Amber Express hybrid, San Joaquin, or Pronto-s hybrid. Other varieties (which require long days—13 hours of sun per day or more) will not do well in Hawai'i.

PREPARATION: Onions do best in a rich, well-drained soil with a pH of 5.5 to 7.0. Add compost or manure to your soil prior to planting. Also, since onions are affected by nematodes, treat the soil prior to planting if nematodes are present.

After preparing your soil with compost or manure, sprinkle about 1 cup of 10-30-10 fertilizer per 10 x 3 feet of onion garden space, and work into the soil.

PLANTING: Plant individual onion sets about 2 inches deep and 3 to 4 inches apart. Cover with soil and water lightly.

WATERING AND WEEDING: Since onions have shallow roots, they need constant moisture, so keep soil slightly damp and water plants lightly when the top of the soil becomes dry. (Insufficient moisture causes the onion bulbs to split.)

Keep your onion garden weed-free by pulling young weeds as they appear, and by hoeing between rows. Remember that onions cannot compete with weeds.

FERTILIZING: When the onion plant's green stems are about 12 inches tall, scatter $1/4$ cup of 10-30-10 fertilizer for every 10 feet of row in a line along the edge of your plants; work into soil carefully.

HARVESTING: When the tops begin to turn yellow, bend them over with the end of a rake. This will stop the growth and allow the bulbs to mature. Stop watering plants at this time. A few days later, when the tops are brown, dig up the bulbs and allow them to dry in the sun for a few days. Cut off the dry tops about 1 inch from the bulb. Store bulbs in a cool, dry place.

EATING: Serve raw, thinly sliced, on sandwiches or in fresh green salads. Add to your favorite stir-fry dish. Place thick onion slices on the barbeque grill and brush lightly with olive oil; grill until golden brown.

FRENCH-FRIED ONION RINGS

Serves 6 to 8

4 large round onions
1 cup milk
2 teaspoons salt
1 cup flour
2 cups shortening

Peel dried skins from onions and discard. Cut onions into $1/4$-inch-thick slices,
then separate into individual rings.
Mix milk with salt. Add onion rings and let stand a few minutes.
Place flour in paper or plastic bag.
Drop onion rings into bag and shake until onion rings are well coated.
Heat shortening in heavy saucepan until it is nearly smoking-hot. Carefully drop
in a few onion rings at a time and fry until they are lightly browned.
Drain fried onion rings on paper towels and sprinkle with additional salt if desired.
Serve immediately.

OLD FASHIONED CLAM CHOWDER

Serves 4 to 6

$1/3$ cup diced salt pork
$2/3$ cup diced, cooked ham
1 tablespoon butter
3 cups chopped onion (about 2 onions)
$3/4$ cup crushed Hilo crackers (4 crackers)
2 cans (6.5 oz. each) chopped clams
3 cups diced potatoes (about 2 potatoes)
1 bay leaf
1 cup milk
1 cup cream
Salt and pepper

Soak salt pork in a cup of water for 5 minutes; drain. In large saucepan sauté salt
pork and ham with butter for several minutes. Add onion; cover and cook slowly
8 to 10 minutes, until onion is tender and translucent. Add crushed crackers.
Drain clams, saving juice. Set clams aside. Add enough water to clam juice to
make 4 cups; pour into onion mixture.
Add potatoes and bay leaf. Stir well; simmer, loosely covered, for 20 minutes.
Stir in clams, milk, and cream. Heat to just below boiling.
Add salt and pepper to taste.

Note: For best flavor, cool, then cover and refrigerate soup for several hours or
overnight; reheat, but do not boil.

A good source of protein and the B-complex vitamins, green peas are a versatile and popular vegetable.

REQUIREMENTS: Like edible-pod Chinese peas, green peas prefer a cooler climate. Consider planting during your cooler months or in partial shade.

PREPARATION: Peas grow best in soil with a pH of 6.0 to 7.5. Soak the seeds in water the night before planting to aid germination. Prepare soil by forking in $1/4$ cup of 10-20-20 fertilizer for every 10 x 10 feet of garden space.

PLANTING: Plant seeds 2 inches deep and 2 inches apart in rows 8 inches apart. Cover with soil and water lightly. Place a trellis down the middle of 2 rows for the vines to climb on.

WATERING AND WEEDING: Water peas when the top of the soil becomes dry. Keep bed weed-free by gently hand-pulling new weeds. If the weather is exceptionally warm, mulch the area to conserve the moisture in the soil and to aid in weed control. When plants begin to bloom, water often to prevent the top of the soil from drying.

HARVESTING: Begin harvesting about 3 weeks after the plant blooms, when the pea pod is plump and bright green. Do not allow peas to overripen; check your crop daily. Pea vines are delicate; to harvest, hold the vine with one hand and pick the pod with the other hand, or cut the pods off with scissors. Your vine may stop producing if you harvest the pod when it is overripe or if you pull the vine while harvesting.

After harvesting is complete, break off vines at ground level, leaving the nitrogen-rich roots in the bed to improve the soil.

EATING: Eat your green peas as soon after harvest as possible, since peas, like corn, quickly lose taste and texture quality after picking. Although my kindergarten teacher ate her peas raw (I was horrified!), most people prefer them lightly steamed.

SPICY PORK AND PEAS
Serves 4 to 6

1 cup fresh peas (in the pod)
1 pound boneless pork, cut into 2-inch x $^1/_2$-inch strips
$^2/_3$ cup bottled stir-fry sauce
3 tablespoons olive or vegetable oil
2 tablespoons minced garlic
2 cups shredded cabbage
1 cup fresh peas
1 cup thinly sliced carrots
1 $^1/_2$ tablespoons Chinese garlic chili sauce
2 tablespoons fresh Chinese parsley (cilantro), chopped
1 5-ounce can crisp chow mein noodles

Steam peas until just tender, about 4 minutes. Set aside.
Marinate pork in 2 tablespoons of the stir-fry sauce for about 15 minutes.
Heat 2 tablespoons oil in large fry pan. Add pork and garlic; fry until meat is just
done, about 4 minutes. Place meat in side dish.
Add remaining 1 tablespoon oil to fry pan; add cabbage, peas, and carrots.
Stir-fry about 3 minutes. Add pork, remaining stir-fry sauce, and Chinese garlic
chili sauce. Stir-fry for 1 minute. Toss with Chinese parsley.
Serve immediately over chow mein noodles.

STEAK IN SOUR CREAM
Serves 2 to 3

1 pound sirloin or round steak
$^1/_4$ cup flour
$^1/_2$ teaspoon seasoned salt
$^1/_2$ teaspoon garlic powder
$^1/_4$ teaspoon pepper
2 tablespoons vegetable or salad oil
1 cup chopped onion
1 cup beef bouillon or broth
$^1/_2$ teaspoon thyme
1 4-ounce can sliced mushrooms (with liquid)
1 cup fresh peas
$^1/_2$ cup sour cream, regular or light

Slice meat into thin, narrow strips. Mix salt, pepper, and garlic powder with
flour. Dredge meat in flour mixture. Heat oil in large frying pan; sauté meat and
onions in pan for 2 to 3 minutes, until meat is browned. Add broth, thyme,
mushrooms with liquid, and peas. Cover and cook 5 to 7 minutes.
Stir in sour cream and heat thoroughly, but do not boil.
Serve over hot rice.

Green, red, and yellow peppers (often called sweet or bell peppers) are all grown the same way; their color is just an indication of their ripeness. And in Hawai'i, where these flavor-packed peppers command such a high price at the supermarket, it is well worth the effort to grow them in your garden. Don't forget that sweet peppers are very high in vitamin C (with about twice as much vitamin C as an orange, in fact).

PEPPERS (SWEET)

REQUIREMENTS: Peppers grow well anywhere in Hawai'i. If space is a problem in your garden, consider growing your peppers in a container.

Peppers grow best in soil with a pH of 5.5 to 7.0 and need 60 to 80 consistently warm days. If you live in the cooler areas of our state, plant your peppers in June or July for a September or October harvest.

PREPARATION: Prepare the soil by scattering 10-20-20 fertilizer over the plot (about 1 cup for a 5- x 10-foot area), adding compost, and working both in well. If cutworms are a problem in your garden, spray plot with Sevin or Diazinon a few days before planting seeds. USE EXTREME CARE WHEN USING PESTICIDES AND READ AND FOLLOW PACKAGE INSTRUCTIONS AND WARNINGS CAREFULLY.

PLANTING: Plant seeds $1/2$ inch deep, 18 to 24 inches apart, in rows 2 feet apart. Cover with soil; tamp lightly with the palm of your hand. Water.

WATERING AND WEEDING: Water deeply when soil becomes dry, being careful not to wet leaves. Pull weeds by hand, as needed.

FERTILIZING: Fertilize with 10-20-20 commercial fertilizer, or manure tea, when plants are about 1 foot tall. Do not fertilize again or the plant will concentrate on developing more leaves and will not flower and fruit.

HARVESTING: To harvest, pick fruit at any stage you choose. When picking, cut, rather than pull, the stem off, to prevent branch breakage. If you want the sweeter-tasting red or yellow peppers, wait until the fruit turns color before you harvest. Continue to harvest peppers to encourage new flowering and fruiting.

EATING: Serve raw in salads, or stir-fry with other vegetables.

PEPPER-CHEESE BAKE
Serves 8

1 ¹/₂ cups raw bulgur
1 ¹/₂ cups boiling water
1 ¹/₂ cups chopped onions
3 tablespoons butter
4 cups minced green peppers
2 cups sliced fresh mushrooms
2 tablespoons dry sherry
1 teaspoon ground marjoram
¹/₄ teaspoon ground pepper
1 ¹/₂ cups cottage cheese
1 cup (8 ounces) feta cheese, crumbled
4 eggs, slightly beaten
¹/₂ teaspoon paprika

Soak bulgur in boiling water for 15 minutes.
Meanwhile, sauté onions in butter until tender.
Add peppers and mushrooms; sauté until peppers are just tender.
Remove from heat and add sherry, marjoram, and ground pepper. Mix well.
Spread bulgur in a buttered 9- x 13- x 2-inch baking dish.
Pour pepper mixture over bulgur.
Mix cottage cheese and feta together; spread over peppers.
Pour beaten eggs over cheese mixture. Sprinkle with paprika.
Bake, uncovered, at 350 degrees for 45 minutes.
Remove from oven and let stand for 10 to 15 minutes before serving.

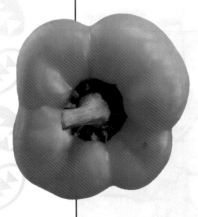

SOUTHERN COLESLAW
Serves 8 to 10

1 head cabbage (about 3 pounds)
1 medium green pepper, chopped fine
1 red onion, chopped fine
1 cup cider vinegar
1 teaspoon salt
1 teaspoon celery seed
1 cup sugar
²/₃ cup salad oil
1 teaspoon dry mustard

Slice cabbage very fine. Combine with green pepper and onion in serving bowl.
Combine remaining ingredients in saucepan. Bring to a boil.
Pour over cabbage mixture, tossing well. Cover and chill overnight.

Known as chayote in Mexican cooking, pipinola (also called pipinella) is a mild-tasting, squashlike fruit high in vitamin C. Pipinola is easy to grow here in Hawai'i, thriving in our warm, semitropical atmosphere. Best yet, pipinola is simple to cook.

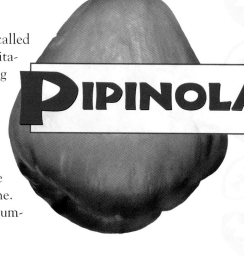

PIPINOLA

SELECTION: The fruit is light green and about the size and shape of a pear. The vine it grows on is started from the sprouting of a mature fruit. Use a fruit from the wild or from a local grocery store to start your own vine. The best time to find pipinola in the stores is in late summer and early fall.

PREPARATION: Prepare a garden area by mixing soil with compost, or lightly sprinkle with 10-30-10 fertilizer and work in. (Note: Too much fertilizer will produce a vine with many leaves but no fruit.)

PLANTING: Place the ripe pipinola in your garden area lengthwise, spacing the fruit about 8 feet apart. Almost cover the fruit with soil. Water lightly. Then, DO NOT WATER again until you see the sprout of the green vine emerge. Pipinola is highly susceptible to rotting, so it is very important that the unsprouted fruit not be kept in soil that is too moist.
    The vine will need to be trellised for support.

WATERING: Water the vine from below and only when the soil has dried.

HARVESTING: Harvest the fruits when firm and before the bottom of the fruit begins to split open.
    Store the freshly harvested pipinola in a plastic bag and refrigerate until ready for use.

EATING: Use as you would other squashes, in soups or stews. Many Mexican cookbooks have recipes for pipinola (chayote).

MEXICAN VEGETABLE SAUTÉ
Serves 6 to 8

$1/4$ cup butter or margarine
1 medium onion, chopped
2 tablespoons minced garlic
3 small zucchini, cut in $1/4$-inch strips
2 medium pipinola, peeled, seeded, and cut in $1/2$-inch cubes
2 small yellow summer squash, cut in $1/2$-inch cubes
$1/2$ cup chopped red bell pepper
$1/2$ cup chopped yellow bell pepper
$1/2$ teaspoon salt
$1/2$ teaspoon cayenne

Melt butter; sauté with onion and garlic until onion is tender.
Add remaining ingredients.
Sauté over high heat until vegetables are crisp-tender.
Serve immediately.

STEAMED PIPINOLA
Serves 3 to 4

2 pipinola
2 tablespoons butter or margarine
1 teaspoon lemon juice

Wash, peel, and cut pipinola into quarters; remove seed portion and discard.
Place quarters in microwave dish.
Cover and microwave on high 6 to 8 minutes.
Toss with butter and lemon juice. Serve hot.

Easy to grow, a good source of vitamin C, and delicious cooked freshly dug from the garden, potatoes should be a part of every Hawai'i vegetable garden.

REQUIREMENTS: Potatoes take a little bit more room than most other garden plants, but if space is a problem, here's a hint: plant about 4 "seed" potatoes (described under SELECTION and PREPARATION, below), and place an old automobile tire around each group of seeds. As the plants grow, cover all but a few leaves with soil, stacking another tire, and then another tire, as needed, as your mound grows higher. To harvest, simply remove tires, then soil, from your tall mound of potatoes. Or plant in a deep-sided container, starting with about 6 to 8 inches of soil below your "seeds," and add soil to the container as the plant grows.

In the hotter areas of our islands, plant potatoes as a winter crop only. Potatoes like sun, cooler weather, and a well-drained acid soil (a pH of 5.0 to 5.5). An acid soil helps prevent a potato disease called "scab." Rotate crops each planting to avoid diseases.

SELECTION: Buy "seed potatoes" from your local nursery. Yes, it is possible to grow plants from potatoes bought at the market. However, most market potatoes, like garlic, have been treated to prevent sprouting. Tubers grown from market potatoes are much smaller and produce a smaller crop. Seed potatoes are more productive, as well as disease-resistant. Use them!

Several varieties of seed potatoes are available. The Red La Soda, found in local nurseries, does well in our warmer climate.

PREPARATION: To prepare "seeds" for planting, cut into pieces, each with 1 or 2 "eyes," or sprouts. To prevent the cut pieces from rotting, cure them by placing them in a bright, airy area or in sunlight for several hours. When cured, they should be slightly dry, and the areas that were cut should have hardened. Sprinkle seeds with sulfur if your climate is particularly wet.

Till soil to a depth of about 7 inches, adding about $^{1}/_{4}$ cup of 10-30-10 fertilizer per 4 x 4 feet of garden space, or per hill.

PLANTING: Plant potatoes in either rows or "hills." Make rows about 3 feet apart, hills about 1 foot apart. Additional fertilizing is not necessary.

To plant in rows: Make a row about 7 inches deep and sprinkle with 10-30-10 fertilizer in the furrow (1 pound per 15 feet of row). Cover with about 3 inches of soil. Place prepared "seeds" in the furrow, spacing them 6 inches apart, and cover with about 4 inches of soil. Water lightly.

To plant in hills: Sprinkle about $^{1}/_{4}$ cup of 10-30-10 fertilizer over a 4-foot area. Form a hill of soil 3 to 4 feet wide and 4 inches high over the fertilizer. Place "seeds" 6 inches apart around the center of the hill and cover with about 4 inches of soil. Water lightly.

As the plants grow, hill soil over the base of the plants and many of the leaves. Continue to do this until the plants blossom. Covering most of the plant with soil will prevent the growing tubers from being exposed to sunlight as well as encourage further root development. If a tuber is exposed to sunlight, the skin will turn green and the potato will be mildly toxic.

WATERING AND WEEDING: Continue to water weekly as the plant grows, to maintain an even moisture level. Otherwise, leaves will droop from lack of moisture, hindering the healthy growth of the plant. Weed carefully.

HARVESTING: When the potato vines begin to wither and brown after flowering, the tubers below are ready for harvest. When the vines have died back, harvest the tubers by carefully digging with your hands or spading fork. Be careful not to nick the tubers. Bruised potatoes do not store well and must be eaten as soon as possible.

EATING: Boil, steam, bake, fry, deep-fry, add to soups and stews; the uses for potatoes are endless!

HOT POTATO SALAD
Serves 4 to 6

2 cups boiled potatoes, diced
1 cup celery, diced
1 can shrimp, drained
1 cup chopped onion
1 can crabmeat, drained
1 cup mayonnaise
1 teaspoon salt
1 tablespoon dried parsley flakes

Mix together all ingredients except parsley. Pour into buttered 9- x 13- x 2-inch casserole dish. Sprinkle top with parsley. Bake for 10 minutes at 450 degrees. Then broil for 3 to 5 minutes, until top has browned.

ROSEMARY POTATOES
Serves 4

2 tablespoons olive oil
2 tablespoons minced garlic
2 teaspoons fresh rosemary leaves
6 cups peeled, cubed potatoes
$1/_2$ teaspoon salt
$1/_4$ teaspoon ground pepper

In large skillet, sauté garlic and rosemary in oil for 1 minute over medium heat. Add remaining ingredients. Sauté for 5 minutes, stirring occasionally. Reduce heat to low; continue cooking, turning potatoes often, until crisp and brown, about 25 minutes.

Perhaps one of the easiest, and thus most rewarding vegetables for a gardener to plant is the common red radish.

RADISHES

REQUIREMENTS: The radish does not do well in extreme heat, so in the hotter areas of Hawai'i be sure to plant and harvest radishes in the cooler months or plant in partial shade, and do not allow the soil to dry out. Radishes will also do well grown in containers, since you can move the container out of the hot noonday sun if necessary.

Radishes do well in almost any soil, but light soils with a pH of 5.5 to 6.8 are best.

PREPARATION: When preparing the soil for planting, remove as many clods, pebbles, and stones as possible, since these obstacles will cause uneven planting depth and prevent uniform germination. The lack of debris in the soil also helps the radish roots to form into a uniform size and shape. Weeds rob radishes of nutrients and moisture. Have your soil as weed-free as possible before planting, since pulling weeds out after the radish plants begin to grow can damage or destroy the plants.

Sprinkle a small amount of 10-20-20 fertilizer over the prepared soil ($^1/_4$ cup of fertilizer for a 2- x 8-foot bed) and work into the soil 1 to 2 inches deep. Radishes need an immediate supply of nutrients to allow them to grow quickly, since they mature in 3 to 4 weeks from the day the seed is first planted. Because this is a root crop, do not use a fertilizer high in nitrogen (the first number in the fertilizer title). Otherwise the plants will be all top, with little or no root. After this initial application of fertilizer, no other fertilizer is needed.

PLANTING: After working fertilizer into the soil, sprinkle the radish seeds very sparingly over the prepared area in rows about 4 to 6 inches apart. Cover the seeds by rubbing soil through the palms of your hands until you have created a layer of soil over the seeds about $^1/_4$ inch deep. Pat soil down lightly. Water the new seedbed gently but thoroughly.

Seeds should germinate in about 5 days. Because of their quick germination, you may consider using radish seeds as "markers" for slower-germinating vegetables. Thin the radish plants soon after germination, so the plants are spaced about 1 $^1/_2$ inches apart. Thinning soon after germination helps prevent the remaining plants from being damaged when you remove the excess plants.

WATERING AND WEEDING: Keep the radish bed moist at all times to allow for even growth of the roots. The drying out of the soil causes poorly formed or cracked radishes of poor quality.

If weeds become a problem, use a hoe to carefully scrape and remove the weeds, since pulling weeds out by the roots may disturb the radish roots as well.

HARVESTING: Harvest your radish crop in 3 to 4 weeks. Carefully pull up the entire plant by grasping the stem with your fingers just above the radish bulb. Radishes can be left in the ground for several days after they mature. However, do not leave them in too long or they will split.

For a continuous supply of radishes throughout the season or year, consider planting a small crop every 14 days or so. You can then harvest a fresh supply of red radishes on a regular basis.

EATING: Serve fresh, as a pupu, dipping lightly into salt just before eating if desired, or slice into green salads or macaroni salad.

RADISH AND VEGETABLE HOT-AND-SOUR SOUP
Serves 4 to 6

5 cups water
5 chicken bouillon cubes
1/4 cup rice wine vinegar
2 tablespoons sugar
1/2 teaspoon finely grated gingerroot (peeled)
1/4 teaspoon ground Cayenne pepper
1 pound (22 count) raw shrimp, shelled and deveined
1 1/2 cups sliced red radishes
1 1/2 cups shredded chopped spinach or Swiss chard leaves
3/4 cup green onions, sliced into 1/2-inch pieces

Combine water and bouillon cubes in large soup pot.
Bring to a boil over high heat. Stir in vinegar, sugar, ginger, and red pepper.
Add shrimp and cook until shrimp turn pink and curl, about 4 minutes.
Remove from heat; stir in radishes, spinach or Swiss chard, and green onions.
Cover and let stand 2 to 3 minutes before serving. Serve hot.

RED RADISH SALAD
Serves 4 to 6

1 dozen red radishes, sliced very thin
1/2 cup onion, finely chopped
2 green onions, chopped

Dressing:
2 tablespoons sour cream
1 tablespoon rice vinegar
2 teaspoons honey
1/2 teaspoon salt
1/4 teaspoon ground pepper

Combine radishes and onions.
Combine dressing ingredients. Add radish mixture to dressing and toss well.
Cover and let stand at room temperature for 1 hour. Stir and serve.

A relative of the onion, shallots taste like a mild-tasting cross between an onion and garlic. Although shallots take 4 to 5 months to mature, the growing time is well worth the wait and garden space, since shallots are very expensive at the supermarket.

SHALLOTS

REQUIREMENTS: Shallots require full sun for at least half the day, a well-drained soil, and a soil pH of 6.0 to 6.5. Like onions, shallots do better at the start, when the green tops are growing, in cooler weather, then like warmer weather for bulb formation. Plan your planting according to your particular weather pattern to accommodate the shallots' needs.

SELECTION: Initially, buy clove starters from your local nursery. After your first harvest, propagate future shallots by simply breaking apart bulb clusters you have harvested and replanting some of the smaller cloves you do not use for cooking. Each clove planted will produce a bulb with up to 8 cloves.

PREPARATION: When preparing your soil for planting, add compost but avoid fresh manure. The nitrogen in the fresh manure will cause your shallots to grow lush green tops at the expense of the desired bulbs. Also avoid highly acid soils. After preparation of the soil, there is no need to fertilize again during the growth of the shallots.

Work your soil deep, to about 8 inches, since the shallot has long roots. Plant cloves 3 to 4 inches apart, root end down, with the tip of the clove barely covered with soil; tamp lightly.

WATERING AND WEEDING: Water after planting; then keep the soil slightly moist. Avoid letting the soil dry out at any time.

Keep your shallots weed-free for best results. Since the shallot's roots are delicate, cut off weeds, since pulling or digging them out may injure the shallot roots.

HARVESTING: As the green tops grow, harvest a few tops by cutting them off near ground level and use them for "chives." New growth of green tops from the center of each plant will stop when the shallot bulbs begin to form below. After about 90 days, expose the new bulbs slightly by drawing the soil away.

When the tops begin to turn yellow, bend them over to stop the sap from going to the tips and allow the plants' energy to concentrate on maturing the bulbs. When the tops are brown a few days later, dig up the bulbs and leave them in the sun to dry, laying the dried tops of one bulb over another bulb to avoid sun scald. When the outside skins are dry, dust off all soil and break or cut off the tops. Store in a cool, dry place until ready to use.

EATING: Chop and serve fresh as you would green onions or garlic, or add to your favorite recipe.

PASTA IN WHITE CLAM SAUCE
Serves 3 to 4

12 ounces spaghetti
$1/2$ cup dry white wine
$1/3$ cup shallots, chopped
1 tablespoon garlic, minced
2 6 $1/2$-ounce cans minced clams
1 cup milk
1 tablespoon flour dissolved in
2 tablespoons water

2 tablespoons grated Parmesan cheese
1 teaspoon dried oregano leaves
3 tablespoons chopped fresh basil
$1/4$ teaspoon ground pepper
$1/2$ teaspoon Tabasco
2 tablespoons chopped fresh parsley

Cook spaghetti according to package directions.
While spaghetti is cooking, prepare sauce:
Place wine, shallots, and garlic in skillet; bring to a boil. Drain clams and pour
reserved clam juice into skillet.
Continue to boil, stirring occasionally, until liquid is reduced to about half,
about 5 minutes. Whisk in milk and dissolved flour mixture,
cooking and whisking until slightly thickened, about 2 minutes.
Add reserved clams and remaining ingredients. Heat 1 minute.
Drain spaghetti. Toss with sauce and serve.

SEARED 'AHI
Serves 4 to 6

2 logs 'ahi, each about 6 inches long
by 1 $1/4$ inches square
$1/3$ cup olive oil
2 tablespoons lemon juice
1 tablespoon finely minced shallots
1 tablespoon grated gingerroot, peeled
1 tablespoon red pepper flakes,
crushed

1 tablespoon finely minced garlic
1 teaspoon dried thyme leaves,
crushed
1 teaspoon dried marjoram leaves,
crushed
1 teaspoon salt
1 teaspoon ground chili powder

Mix together all ingredients except 'ahi in shallow bowl.
Dredge 'ahi logs in spice mixture. Let stand 5 minutes.
Heat wok or frying pan until very hot.
Sear each 'ahi log for 20 seconds on each of its 4 sides.
Remove from heat. Slice logs diagonally into $1/2$-inch slices.
Serve immediately with wasabi sauce.

WASABI SAUCE

$1/4$ cup shoyu
1 tablespoon mirin
1 tablespoon lemon juice

1 teaspoon wasabi paste
$1/2$ teaspoon sesame seeds

Mix shoyu with wasabi paste until well blended. Add remaining ingredients and
mix well. Serve as dipping sauce for seared 'ahi.

Spinach is high in vitamins A and C, calcium, and iron.

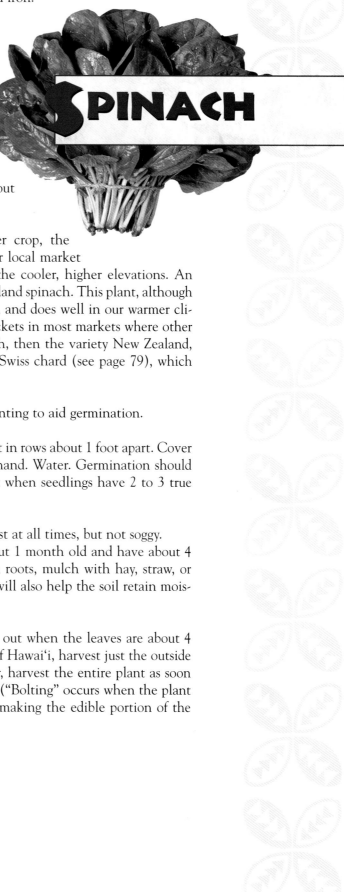

REQUIREMENTS: Spinach prefers a slightly acidic soil, with an ideal pH of 6.0 to 6.5. Plant in the winter months, November through January, to harvest before the warm spring and summer begins. If you feel the weather is still too warm, plant spinach in the shade of other, taller crops in your garden. Spinach thrives on nitrogen, so the addition of bone meal, blood meal, or fish scraps to the soil prior to planting is beneficial. Work these in well with compost to a depth of about 1 foot.

SELECTION: Because spinach is a cool-weather crop, the spinach varieties you may be familiar with in your local market do not grow well in most of Hawai'i, except in the cooler, higher elevations. An excellent spinach for your home garden is New Zealand spinach. This plant, although not a true spinach, has smooth, light green leaves, and does well in our warmer climate. You will find New Zealand Spinach seed packets in most markets where other seeds are found. Look for a packet labeled Spinach, then the variety New Zealand, usually in parentheses. Another fine substitute is Swiss chard (see page 79), which may be used in any recipes calling for spinach.

PREPARATION: Soak seeds overnight before planting to aid germination.

PLANTING: Plant $^1/_2$ inch deep and 2 inches apart in rows about 1 foot apart. Cover with soil and tamp lightly with the palm of your hand. Water. Germination should occur within 10 days. Thin to 4 to 6 inches apart when seedlings have 2 to 3 true leaves.

WATERING AND FERTILIZING: Keep soil moist at all times, but not soggy.

Fertilize with manure tea when plants are about 1 month old and have about 4 true leaves. Since weeding may harm the spinach roots, mulch with hay, straw, or grass clippings to keep weeds under control. This will also help the soil retain moisture.

HARVESTING: To harvest, pull the entire plant out when the leaves are about 4 inches long. If you live in one of the cooler areas of Hawai'i, harvest just the outside leaves to extend the plants' productivity. However, harvest the entire plant as soon as there is any sign that the plant is ready to bolt. ("Bolting" occurs when the plant quickly goes to the flowering or seed stage, often making the edible portion of the plant tough and bitter.)

ROMAN SPINACH
Serves 3 to 4

4 cups spinach
3 strips bacon, diced
$1/3$ cup raisins
3 tablespoons pine nuts
2 tablespoons minced garlic
$1/2$ teaspoon salt
$1/4$ teaspoon ground pepper

Steam spinach until very wilted, about 10 minutes; drain.
Sauté bacon until crisp. Add raisins, pine nuts, garlic, salt, and pepper.
Sauté about 3 minutes, until garlic is lightly browned.
Add spinach, tossing to mix well. Sauté 2 minutes.
Serve immediately.

SPINACH-ORANGE SALAD

4 cups fresh spinach leaves or chard leaves
1 can mandarin oranges, drained
$1/2$ cup sliced red onion
$1/4$ cup slivered almonds
3 tablespoons white vinegar
2 tablespoons salad oil
4 slices bacon, fried and crumbled
1 tablespoon honey
$1/2$ teaspoon salt

Remove coarse stems from spinach; wash and dry leaves.
Tear spinach leaves into bite-sized pieces and place in a serving bowl.
Add oranges and onions.
Mix remaining ingredients. Pour over spinach.
Toss gently and serve.

Squash is a good source of vitamin A, potassium, and phosphorus, and is a versatile vegetable in the kitchen.

SQUASH

REQUIREMENTS: Squash, whether it is zucchini, yellow crookneck, Italian, acorn, or pumpkin, grows well almost anywhere in Hawai'i. Remember, though, that squash plants require a lot of garden space to grow.

Squash prefers full sun, a well-drained soil, and a pH of 6.0 to 7.0. Since the squash vines are susceptible to nematode damage, treat soil prior to planting if nematodes are present.

PREPARATION: Prepare the soil by working in compost or well-rotted manure. Work in $1/_2$ cup of 10-20-20 fertilizer for every 12 square feet of garden area to be planted.

PLANTING: Plant seeds 1 inch deep. Plant bush variety seeds 2 to 3 feet apart in rows 4 to 6 feet apart. Plant vine varieties 3 to 4 feet apart in rows 8 to 10 feet apart. Water seeds deeply after planting. Two to 3 vines should be sufficient to produce enough squash to feed 4 people.

You can also plant bush varieties in hills spaced 4 to 5 feet apart, spacing 3 to 4 seeds about 6 inches apart in each hill. The hills for vine varieties should be spaced about 10 feet apart.

WATERING AND WEEDING: Squash plants have a shallow root system, so weed carefully. As plants grow, mulch with dry straw or leaves to control weeds and keep water from evaporating. Do not allow the soil to dry out. When watering, be careful to water only the soil, not the vines, to help prevent diseases.

As squash mature, place a board or thick mulch under each fruit to prevent rot.

PEST CONTROL: Insects can be a major problem for squash. Remember, however, that bees are necessary for pollination. Therefore, use insecticides only in the late afternoon, when bees are less likely to be around the plants and the squash flowers are no longer fresh. Use an insecticidal soap or general garden dust to help control insect infestation. Diazinon or Malathion will control most severe infestations. USE EXTREME CARE WHEN USING PESTICIDES AND READ AND FOLLOW PACKAGE INSTRUCTIONS AND WARNINGS CAREFULLY.

FERTILIZING: When fruit first begins to appear on the vine, fertilize each plant with manure tea or carefully work into the soil 2 tablespoons of 10-20-20 per plant.

HARVESTING: Summer squash varieties (such as yellow crookneck and zucchini) are ready to harvest about 60 days after planting. Winter varieties (such as acorn and pumpkin) may take more than 100 days to mature.

Harvest summer squash before it is quite fully ripe, just as the old blossom drops off the tip. The skin and flesh should be tender and succulent. Fruit should be easily punctured.

Winter squash will have a watery, bland taste if not allowed to mature on the vine. Wait until the shells of winter squash are hard and the vines have died back before harvesting. Let harvested winter squash cure in the sun for about a week before storing in a cool, dry place.

Harvest both summer and winter squash by cutting the fruit off the vine with a sharp knife. Pulling the fruit off the vine or carrying squash by their stems damages the stem. A squash will quickly rot if the stem has been damaged.

EATING: Steam or stir-fry with other vegetables, or add to soups or stews. Serve zucchini raw, sliced thin, with your favorite dip.

PASTA PRIMAVERA
(Kimberly's favorite, and a vegetarian delight)
Serves 4

12 ounces uncooked linguine or spaghetti
2 teaspoons vegetable oil
1 medium onion, chopped
1 tablespoon chopped garlic
1 cup sliced yellow crookneck squash
1 cup sliced zucchini
1 cup green or yellow bell pepper strips

1 14 $1/2$-ounce can stewed tomatoes
1 6-ounce can Italian-style tomato paste
$3/4$ cup water
$1/2$ teaspoon salt
$1/4$ teaspoon pepper
2 tablespoons chopped fresh basil
Grated Parmesan cheese (optional)

Boil large pot of water and begin cooking pasta.
Meanwhile, sauté onion and garlic in heated oil for 1 minute;
add squash, zucchini, and bell pepper. Sauté 3 to 4 minutes.
Drain tomatoes and stir reserved tomato juice into squash mixture.
Add tomato paste, water, salt, and pepper. Simmer 5 minutes.
Stir in reserved tomatoes and basil. Simmer 1 minute.
Drain pasta. Serve sauce over pasta.
Sprinkle with grated Parmesan cheese if desired.

STUFFED SQUASH
Serves 4

2 large acorn or butternut squash
1 $1/2$ cups chopped fresh mushrooms
1 cup chopped onion
1 tablespoon minced garlic
2 tablespoons butter
$1/2$ teaspoon salt
$1/4$ teaspoon ground pepper

1 cup cottage cheese
$3/4$ cup cooked rice
$1/4$ cup fresh parsley, chopped
2 tablespoons dry white wine
2 teaspoons fresh chopped basil

Cut squash in half lengthwise; remove seeds. Bake, cut-side down, on a greased
baking sheet, at 350 degrees for $1/2$ hour, or until tender.
Sauté mushrooms, onions, and garlic in butter until onions are tender; drain well,
reserving liquid. Add remaining ingredients, mixing well.
Fill baked squash with mushroom mixture.
Bake, uncovered, at 350 degrees for $1/2$ hour,
basting occasionally with reserved liquid.

Although unrelated, sweet potatoes and yams, both good sources of vitamins A and C and beta carotene, are often used in the kitchen interchangeably, and the plants are grown under similar conditions. The true sweet potato has dry white and purple flesh. The yam has moister, orange flesh. Most vines found in Hawai'i are sweet potatoes. Sweet potatoes are originally from the South American Andes. The cultivation of sweet potatoes in Hawai'i is evidence of the ancient trade across the Pacific Ocean between the Americas and the Pacific Islands.

Sweet Potatoes and Yams

REQUIREMENTS: Sweet potatoes do well in all areas of Hawai'i. They prefer a loose, well-drained soil with a pH of 5.0 to 6.0, preferably free from rocks. A heavy, rock-filled soil produces deformed and misshapen potatoes.

planted March

SELECTION: Sweet potatoes can be planted any time of the year. Obtain vine cuttings from your local nursery or from neighbors.

PREPARATION: Till soil and remove all rocks. Since sweet potatoes are susceptible to nematodes, treat soil prior to planting if nematodes are a problem. Do not add manure, since it may encourage diseases to attack the developing potatoes. Also, avoid a high concentration of nitrogen in the soil or in any fertilizers used, since excess nitrogen causes the vines to grow rather than the roots (potatoes). Excess nitrogen also causes the potatoes to have deep ridges.

less fertilizer

PLANTING: Plant 8 to 12 vine cuttings at an angle in the ground, with about $^2/_3$ of the vine covered with soil. Water deeply after planting and then whenever the soil becomes dry. Space the vines 6 to 12 inches apart in rows about 3 feet apart.

About 3 weeks after planting, side-dress the vines with $^1/_4$ cup of 10-20-20 fertilizer per vine. Dig the fertilizer in about 3 inches deep, about 4 inches to the side of each vine, in 3- to 4-inch lengths.

WATERING AND WEEDING: Weed the garden bed until the vines start crawling; then the vines should pretty much take care of any unwanted weeds.

Do not water for the last 3 to 4 weeks before harvesting. Potatoes are easier to harvest when the soil is dry. Also, if you water after the sweet potatoes have matured, the moisture may cause the potatoes to sprout.

HARVESTING: Sweet potatoes are ready to harvest in 4 to 6 months. Sweet potatoes left in the ground too long will become overlarge and may become susceptible to insect and disease infestation.

To harvest, first be sure the soil is dry so the potatoes will be free of soil. (If it is necessary to dig up the potatoes when the soil is wet, do not wash the potatoes. Instead, place them in a protected area until the soil dries and can be easily brushed off.) Before removing potatoes from the ground, cut the vines off at the base of the soil and save for replanting.

Carefully dig up the sweet potatoes, being careful not to cut or bruise the roots. Place the harvested sweet potatoes in a well-ventilated room or garage for 2 to 3 weeks. This allows any cuts or bruises to heal and also allows some of the starches of the potato to convert to sugar, producing a sweeter flavor. The ideal temperature for such curing of your crop is 85 degrees.

After curing, store the potatoes in a cool, but unrefrigerated area; ideal temperature is 55 to 70 degrees.

EATING: To prepare, cut sweet potatoes into small chunks and place in a shallow bowl. Add about $^1/_4$ inch of water. Cover with plastic wrap and microwave on high for 5 to 7 minutes, until potatoes are tender. Salt and pepper to taste. Add butter, if desired, and serve. They are also great as fried chips. Follow any recipe for homemade potato chips, substituting sweet potatoes or yams for potatoes.

CANDIED SWEET POTATOES
Serves 6 to 8

6 large sweet potatoes
$^1/_4$ cup orange juice
1 tablespoon lemon juice
$^1/_2$ cup brown sugar
$^1/_2$ teaspoon salt
$^1/_4$ teaspoon ground pepper
3 tablespoons butter

Boil sweet potatoes for 15 minutes, or just until tender; drain and slice.
Butter casserole dish; place sliced potatoes in dish.
Combine orange and lemon juices, sugar, salt, and pepper. Pour over potatoes.
Dot with butter. Bake at 400 degrees for 30 minutes, until crisp and brown.

SWEET POTATO WITH COCONUT MILK
Serves 4 to 6

4 to 5 sweet potatoes
$^1/_2$ cup coconut milk
$^1/_2$ cup sweetened condensed milk
$^1/_4$ teaspoon salt
1 cup corn flakes, crushed
1 cup miniature marshmallows

Wash and scrub the skin of the potatoes. Place in a pot and cover with water.
Boil for about 20 minutes, until potatoes are tender. Remove from heat and drain.
Peel potatoes while still warm. Mash.
Combine coconut milk, condensed milk, and salt. Add to mashed potatoes.
Beat with electric mixer until fluffy.
Pour mashed potatoes into a buttered casserole. Sprinkle with corn flakes and top with marshmallows. Bake at 350 degrees until potatoes are heated through and marshmallows are golden brown. Serve immediately.

An excellent substitute for spinach, Swiss chard is high in vitamins A and C and a good source of beta carotene.

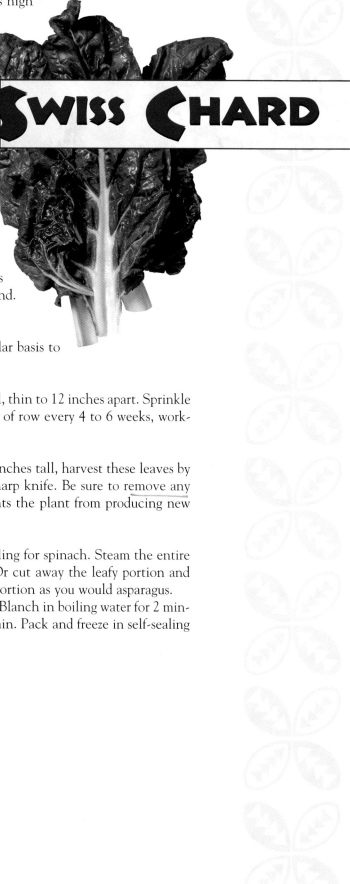

REQUIREMENTS: An easy plant to grow, Swiss chard tolerates a range of soils and temperatures and can be planted at any time during the year. If you live in an area that is very wet, be sure the soil is well drained. Chard prefers a less acid soil, with a pH of 6.5 to 7.5. A single planting can be harvested for 4 to 6 months by simply harvesting the outer leaves as needed. The plant quickly replaces these with new leaves.

PLANTING: Place seeds about 6 inches apart in 1-inch rows 1 $1/_2$ feet apart. Cover rows and seeds with soil and tamp lightly with the palm of your hand. Water lightly.

WATERING: Continue to water plants on a regular basis to keep soil slightly damp.

FERTILIZING: When plants are about 6 inches tall, thin to 12 inches apart. Sprinkle with $1/_4$ cup of 10-30-10 fertilizer per every 10 feet of row every 4 to 6 weeks, working carefully into the soil, or use manure tea.

HARVESTING: When outer leaves are about 10 inches tall, harvest these leaves by cutting them off at the base of the plant with a sharp knife. Be sure to remove any old or tough leaves, since leaving them on prevents the plant from producing new growth.

EATING: Substitute Swiss chard in any recipe calling for spinach. Steam the entire leaf as you would spinach, for 15 to 20 minutes. Or cut away the leafy portion and prepare like spinach; then cook and serve the rib portion as you would asparagus.

To freeze, wash chard and remove heavy stems. Blanch in boiling water for 2 minutes. Remove from water, run under cold water; drain. Pack and freeze in self-sealing plastic bags or freezer containers.

CHICKEN–SWISS CHARD BAKE
Serves 4 to 6

3 tablespoons salad oil
2 tablespoons minced garlic
1 cup chopped onion
3 pounds chicken pieces
1 stalk celery, chopped
2 medium carrots, chopped
1-inch piece gingerroot, sliced into 4 or 5 pieces
1 cup chicken bouillon or stock
3 tablespoons shoyu
$^1/_4$ cup sherry
1 tablespoon brown sugar
2 tablespoons butter
8 ounces fresh mushrooms, sliced
1 tablespoon lemon juice
12 large leaves Swiss chard
4 ounces sliced baked ham, chopped

Sauté onion and garlic in oil in large fry pan; place in large baking pot.
Sauté chicken in same fry pan until chicken is browned; add to pot.
Add celery, carrots, ginger, chicken bouillon, shoyu, sherry, and brown sugar to chicken mixture; mix well. Cover and bake at 350 degrees for $^1/_2$ hour.
Sauté mushrooms in butter in fry pay; add lemon and add to chicken mixture.
Top chicken with Swiss chard and sprinkle with ham.
Cover and bake an additional $^1/_2$ hour. Serve immediately.

LENTIL AND SWISS CHARD SOUP
Serves 4 to 6

1 $^1/_2$ cups lentils
10 cups water
1 tablespoon salt
1 large onion, chopped
1 tablespoon minced garlic
4 tablespoons vegetable or salad oil
2 medium potatoes, diced
2 cups chopped fresh Swiss chard
2 tablespoons lemon juice
$^1/_2$ teaspoon whole coriander, crushed
2 tablespoons red wine vinegar
$^1/_4$ cup chopped green onion

Wash lentils. Soak overnight, changing water several times.
Place lentils in large pot.
Add water and salt; bring to a boil; reduce heat and simmer 1 hour.
Meanwhile, sauté onion and garlic in oil until tender.
Add potatoes, Swiss chard, lemon juice, and coriander, along with onion and garlic, to lentil mixture. Simmer soup another 20 minutes, until potatoes are tender. (Add a little boiling water if soup becomes too thick.)
Just before serving, add wine vinegar. Place in soup bowls and top with green onion. Serve with crackers, if desired.

Upland taro is grown mainly for its leaves, whereas the more familiar wetland taro is grown for both its leaves and its root. This versatile vegetable, high in vitamins A and C, calcium, fiber, and iron, has been a staple of the Hawaiians for centuries.

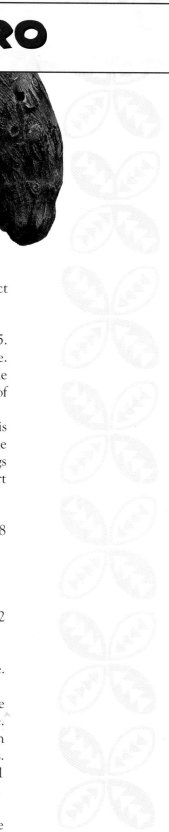

TARO

REQUIREMENTS: Wetland taro must be grown in waterlogged or flooded fields, or fields containing slow-moving water. However, you can grow upland (or dryland) taro in just about any backyard garden here in Hawai'i and harvest taro's delicious leaves without having to flood your yard!

The ideal climate for upland taro is warm and moist, with evenly distributed rainfall. Plant your taro in as sunny a place as possible. Compensate for lack of consistent rainfall by diligently watering your plants. Consider planting taro at the edge of the eaves of your house, where the plants will catch drips.

SELECTION: Two varieties of upland taro grown for the root as well as the leaf are Lehua Maoli and Bun Long. The Lehua Maoli root is great for making poi, and the Bun Long root can be made into taro chips.

Obtain taro plants (huli) from neighbors or from some local nurseries, or contact your local U. H. Cooperative Extension Service for suggestions.

PREPARATION: Upland taro prefers a well-drained soil with a pH of 5.5 to 6.5. Prepare the soil by tilling, removing all weeds and as many stones as possible. Sprinkle 16-16-16 fertilizer, about 1 cup per 50 square feet of garden space, over the prepared soil and work in with a garden fork. Also mix in a substantial amount of compost to make the soil very loose.

You will actually be planting a part of the root (corm) of the taro plant, which is the part that is made into poi. To prepare a cutting for planting, cut off the tip of the corm about 1 inch down from the top, along with a couple of leaves. Let the cuttings (called huli) dry for a day. Or use some of the small side-shoots (called 'ohā) to start your new plant.

PLANTING: To plant, set the taro huli in the ground about 3 inches deep and 18 inches apart in rows 18 to 24 inches apart. Cover with soil. Water deeply.

WATERING AND WEEDING: Keep soil moist at all times. Keep area weed-free.

FERTILIZING: Side-dress with 16-16-16 fertilizer, 1 cup per 50 square feet, every 2 months.

HARVESTING: Leaves may be harvested and used for lū'au or laulau at any time. Harvest only the young leaves, allowing the remainder of the plant to grow.

Upland taro roots are ready to harvest 8 to 12 months after the planting of the huli. When the leaves of the plant begin to turn yellow, it is close to harvest time. Also, the corm, or root, of the taro plant will protrude from the ground. You can then harvest taro roots at your convenience, when needed, for the next several weeks. Wash and drain the corms (roots) prior to storing in the refrigerator. Cut off about 1 inch of the top of each corm and replant this new huli to continue your taro patch.

EATING: Use the harvested taro root as soon as possible to preserve quality. Grate for "hash browns," cut like potatoes for stew, or slice and deep-fry to make crunchy chips.

Use taro leaves as you would cooked spinach. Be sure to cook the taro leaves thoroughly, since they contain calcium oxalate crystals. These crystals, which can cause throat and esophagus swelling, are eliminated by long, slow cooking.

OVEN LAULAU
Serves 8

3 pounds pork butt or similar cut pork roast
1 tablespoon Hawaiian salt
1 pound salted butterfish
3 pounds lūʻau leaves (taro leaves)
6 ti leaves

Debone pork, cut off excess fat, and cut meat into cubes. Add salt and knead into meat well. Scale fish and cut into 1-inch cubes. Soak fish for 2 hours, change water, and soak for another 2 hours.
Wash lūʻau leaves and cut off the tips of the stocks (hāhā). Cut leaves into small pieces.
Wash and debone ti leaves. Line a baking pan with the ti leaves.
Place $1/2$ of the lūʻau leaves on top.
Place meat, then fish, on top of the lūʻau leaves.
Cover all with the remaining lūʻau leaves.
Seal with foil and bake at 350 degrees for 4 hours.

TARO PUDDING
Serves 6 to 8

4 cups grated taro root
$3/4$ cup dark brown sugar
1 cup honey
1 cup canned coconut milk
2 large ti leaves

Mix taro, sugar, honey, and milk together.
Line a loaf pan with foil. Place ti leaves on the foil, cutting to fit the pan.
Pour pudding mixture into the pan and cover with foil.
Bake 2 hours at 400 degrees.
Remove top foil during last $1/2$ hour of baking so pudding can brown.
Cool and serve.

This is probably the most popular vegetable found in backyard gardens.

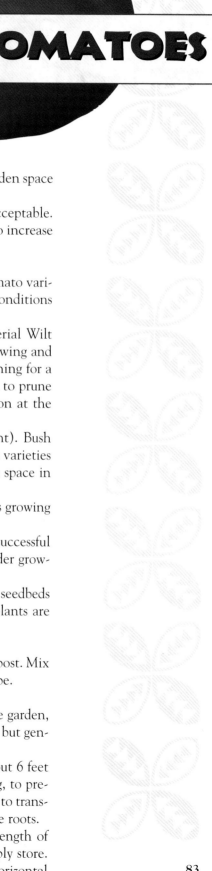

REQUIREMENTS: Tomatoes can be grown successfully, and nearly year-round, almost anywhere in Hawai'i. For a successful tomato crop, it is important to consider the elevation, rainfall, day and night temperatures, soil composition, and existing pests of your particular region.

If you live in the 1,000- to 3,000-foot elevation, you should be able to grow tomatoes year-round. At the warmer elevations—from sea level to about 1,000 feet—plant tomatoes from September through May. And for elevations over 3,000 feet, plant from March through August.

Tomatoes, especially cherry tomatoes, grow well in containers. So, if garden space is a problem, consider growing tomatoes on your lanai.

Ideal soil pH for tomatoes is 6.0 to 6.5, but a pH range of 5.5 to 7.0 is acceptable. If you live in areas with high rainfall, you may need to add lime to the soil to increase the pH as well as the calcium in your soil.

SELECTION: For the greatest success in tomato growing, stick with the tomato varieties developed by the University of Hawai'i. Adapted to the growing conditions throughout our state, the UH hybrids and varieties include the following:

VINES: N-5, N-52, N-63, N-65, N-69, and BWN-21 (which is Bacterial Wilt tolerant). These are "indeterminate tomatoes," which means they keep growing and producing unless stopped by disease. Vine varieties require staking and pruning for a successful crop, but take up less space in your garden. (Note that if you fail to prune the vine varieties, the plant will put too much energy into vine production at the expense of fruit production.)

BUSH: Anahu, Healani, and Kewalo (which is Bacterial Wilt tolerant). Bush tomatoes are "determinate"; they set fruit once and then stop growing. Bush varieties do not require pruning and need only a little staking, but do take up more space in your garden than vine varieties.

The Tropic and Floramerica, both from Florida, are adapted to Hawai'i's growing conditions, but are not nematode resistant.

If uncontrollable pests or other conditions prevent you from growing a successful crop, try the more hardy cherry tomatoes, like Pixie or Tiny Tim. Or consider growing your tomatoes in containers.

Tomatoes can be bought as seedlings from your local nursery, started in seedbeds or flats for later transplanting, or planted directly into the ground. Transplants are usually about 3 to 5 weeks old.

PREPARATION: Prepare your soil by mixing in well-rotted manure or compost. Mix 1 tablespoon 10-20-20 fertilizer into the soil where each tomato plant will be.

PLANTING: When transplanting seedlings to their permanent place in the garden, plant so the lowest set of leaves is at ground level. Press the soil down firmly but gently around the plant and water well.

For vine varieties, space plants about 18 inches apart. Place stakes (about 6 feet tall) or tomato cages in the ground, about 6 inches deep, just after planting, to prevent damaging the roots later on. Space bush varieties about 3 feet apart. Try to transplant your seedlings on a cloudy day and be sure not to disturb their delicate roots.

HINT: To make your own tomato cage: for each cage buy an 8-foot length of welded steel mesh used to reinforce concrete, available at any building supply store. Or use some other type of heavy duty wide-mesh wire. Cut off the bottom horizontal

wire, creating a row of 5-inch tines that you will push into the ground to anchor the cage. Bend the mesh into a circle and, using pliers, twist the clipped ends of the wire around each other to form the cage. Set the cage upright, with the 5-inch tines on the bottom, around each tomato plant.

To plant tomatoes directly into the ground, group 3 or 4 seeds, about 1 inch apart, in one spot, covering with $^1/_2$ inch of soil. Space the groups at the same distances you would tomato seedlings, depending on whether you are planting vine or bush tomatoes. Tamp ground lightly and water gently but well. Keep area slightly moist until seeds germinate, in about 7 to 10 days. When seedlings are about 1 inch tall, leave the strongest seedling, cutting off all others.

WATERING AND WEEDING: Water your tomato seedlings 1 to 2 times a week (if rainfall is very light or absent), until small fruits begin to appear. From that time, water deeply 2 to 3 times a week. Try not to wet the foliage when watering, since wet leaves are more prone to disease. For ease in watering, tie a rag around the outlet of your garden hose and turn the water on as slowly as possible. Lay the hose next to the tomato plant and allow the water to soak deeply into the soil. The rag prevents the water pressure from the hose from digging a hole in your soil. Note that lack of soil moisture causes blossom end rot (a water-soaked spot near the blossom end, or bottom, of the tomato that appears when the fruit is about $^1/_3$ developed). An even moisture supply also helps prevent the cracking of the fruit.

Mulch your plants with grass clippings or old hay to keep your tomatoes from touching the soil and to prevent blossom end rot. Mulching also holds in soil moisture and controls weed growth.

Keep the area around your tomato plants weed-free by pulling weeds by hand, thus preventing damage to the tomato roots.

PRUNING AND STAKING: As vine plants grow, prune each plant by snapping off the sprouts that grow between the main stem and the leaf axils, leaving only 1 or 2 central shoots. Then tie the vines loosely to the stakes, or cages, at about 12-inch intervals, with strips of cloth or raffia, twist ties, pieces of pantyhose, or other soft tying material.

FERTILIZING: When the first fruit begins to appear, fertilize each plant with $^1/_4$ cup of 10-20-20 fertilizer, applying it in a circle around each plant about 6 inches from the base and carefully scratching the fertilizer into the soil. Repeat every 2 weeks. Or apply manure tea in place of the 10-20-20 fertilizer.

PEST CONTROL: Tomato plants are susceptible to many garden pests. If cutworms are present in your garden, treat soil prior to planting, or place a paper cup with the bottom cut out over each tomato seedling, burying the cup about 1 inch in the ground. To combat other insects, spray with a general purpose tomato spray, available at supermarkets and nurseries, following label directions carefully. Rotate pesticide families to avoid the development of insect resistance. USE EXTREME CARE WHEN USING PESTICIDES AND READ AND FOLLOW PACKAGE INSTRUCTIONS AND WARNINGS CAREFULLY. If pests are too great a problem, try growing the small cherry tomatoes instead. Their flavor is excellent.

Planting dill near tomatoes helps repel pests. Avoid planting tomatoes next to peppers, eggplant, and potatoes, since they are relatives and subject to the same diseases.

Interesting note: tomatoes, eggplant, potatoes, and peppers are related to the tobacco plant and are subject to a disease called tobacco mosaic virus. Because of this, you should not smoke around these plants, and should wash your hands (after smoking) before handling them to avoid spreading the disease.

HARVESTING: Harvesting begins about 70 to 90 days after transplanting. Harvest tomatoes no sooner than when the bottom of the fruit begins to turn pink. Fruits picked fully ripe have a better flavor. Gently twist the fruits off the vine, being careful not to injure the supporting vine. Wash tomatoes carefully with water no cooler than the temperature of the tomato. Otherwise the water may be absorbed by the fruit.

Rotate your tomato crops to prevent the spread of disease. After the final harvest, destroy the tomato vines or place in bags and discard with the household rubbish, again to prevent the spread of disease in your garden.

EATING: Tomatoes are great served fresh, alone or in salads; lightly stir-fried with other vegetables; or cooked into sauces.

FRIED GREEN TOMATOES
Serves 3 to 4

2 green tomatoes (barely pink on the bottom)
1 egg
$1/4$ cup flour or cornmeal
$1/4$ teaspoon pepper
2 tablespoons vegetable oil

Cut tomatoes into $1/4$-inch slices. Beat egg well with fork. Mix flour and pepper.
Dip tomato slices in egg, then in flour. Heat oil in skillet.
Fry floured tomatoes in hot oil until golden brown, about 2 minutes on each side.
Serve immediately.

LOMI SALMON
Serves 8

$1/2$ pound salted salmon
4 green onions, cut into $1/4$-inch slices
1 medium onion, finely chopped
4 large tomatoes, chopped into small pieces

Soak salmon overnight in water.
Remove skin and bones from salmon; break into small pieces.
Combine remaining ingredients with salmon.
Chill well and serve.

Watercress is a fresh-tasting, slightly spicy vegetable, high in vitamin C, not commonly found in backyard gardens.

WATERCRESS

REQUIREMENTS: Watercress is a popular salad plant that is usually grown in slowly running water. However, it will also grow in well-manured soil in a partly shady or shady area, as long as the soil is kept wet. In Hawai'i, watercress will grow all year long. However, it is best grown in the cooler winter months of November through April, since it is sensitive to temperatures over 85 degrees. Even water temperatures over 78 degrees cause slower and poorer growth. Overhead sprinkling with water several times a day during hot days will help preserve your crop.

Watercress needs nitrogen to grow, so an addition of sulfate of ammonia may be advantageous to your crop. Additionally, watercress prefers a pH below 7.5 and a low chloride content in the water. If your crop of watercress is struggling, you may want to have your water source analyzed for its chloride content.

SELECTION: For your planting, use pieces of watercress (obtained from your local supermarket) that have begun to root, or obtain watercress shoots from your local nursery. Note: Avoid watercress that you may find growing in local streams, since it may harbor diseases transmitted to the water by wild pigs and cattle in the area.

PREPARATION: Make a trench 3 feet wide and 1 foot deep. Layer the trench with 6 inches of manure, then 4 inches of soil, then 2 inches of sand.

PLANTING: Plant the already rooting pieces of watercress, each piece about 6 inches long, about 4 inches apart in the sand layer.

Keep the plants saturated with water at all times. Consider planting your watercress near the downspout of your rain gutter. You can then divert the water to your plants to help provide the constant supply of water needed to grow watercress. On Lāna'i we used to pick watercress that was growing next to a huge old wooden water tank down by the boat harbor. For years the old tank had a small leak, and some enterprising resident planted watercress next to the tank. What a wonderful idea! Although this tank was in an extremely arid area, the crop of watercress flourished for years. Amazing what a little water will do.

PEST CONTROL: Occasionally your watercress crop will be bothered by pests. Signs of infestation include stunted and curled shoots (aphids); mottled leaf surface (grass sharpshooter); or wilting and death of the shoot (southern green stink bug). These pests can be controlled by the use of insecticidal soap, a general garden dust, or in severe cases, Diazinon. However, do not use Diazinon within 5 days of harvest. USE EXTREME CARE WHEN USING PESTICIDES AND READ AND FOLLOW PACKAGE INSTRUCTIONS AND WARNINGS CAREFULLY.

HARVESTING: Harvest in 45 to 60 days, when the plants are 12 inches tall. To harvest, grasp the stem with one hand and cut, using a knife or sickle, with the other hand. Remove the lower yellow leaves. Wash well in cool water. Use as soon as possible. To store, place in a damp plastic bag in the refrigerator.

New growth will come from the stems left in the bed after harvesting. You can also plant additional cuttings to ensure a bountiful new crop.

EATING: Fresh, tender watercress can be eaten raw (perhaps with a little mayonnaise or mayonnaise and shoyu mixture); mixed in green salads; or cooked. Watercress is excellent added to a bowl of saimin just before serving. Older, less fresh watercress is best cooked or made into soup stock.

JAPANESE-STYLE WATERCRESS
Serves 4

3/4 pound watercress (a bundle large enough to grasp in your hand),
cut into 1 1/2-inch pieces
2 tablespoons sugar
2 tablespoons shoyu
1 tablespoon mirin
1 tablespoon toasted sesame seeds

Place watercress in a colander. Pour boiling water over watercress. Drain well.
Mix remaining ingredients well; toss with watercress and serve.

WATERCRESS-BEEF SAUTÉ
Serves 4

1/2 pound teriyaki-cut meat, cut into small pieces
2 cups chicken broth
2 teaspoons garlic powder
3/4 pound watercress (a bundle large enough to grasp in your hand),
cut into 3-inch pieces
2 cans water chestnuts, chopped
2 eggs, beaten
2 green onions, chopped

Sauté meat in skillet until browned.
Add broth, garlic powder, watercress, and water chestnuts. Bring to a boil.
Add eggs and mix thoroughly.
Add green onions; lower heat and simmer 1 minute. Serve over rice.
Makes 4 servings.

BIBLIOGRAPHY

Better Homes and Gardens. *Vegetables and Herbs You Can Grow*. Des Moines, Iowa: Meredith Corporation, 1978.

Bio-Control of the Spiraling Whitefly. Hawai'i State Department of Agriculture, Biological Control Section, Plant Pest Control Branch, June 1980; rev. October 1980.

Bradley, Fern Marshall, and Barbara W. Ellis, eds. *Rodale's All-New Encyclopedia of Organic Gardening*. Emmaus, PA: Rodale Press, 1992.

Brewbaker, James L. *Hawaii H38 and Hawaii H68: Hawaiian Sweet Corn Hybrids*. University of Hawai'i Agricultural Experiment Station, Circular #66, June 1968.

Brewbaker, James L., and Yukio Nakagawa. *Sweet Corn*. University of Hawai'i Cooperative Extension Service, Home Garden Vegetable Series #4, March 1978.

Calkins, Carroll, ed. *The* Reader's Digest *Illustrated Guide to Gardening*. New York: Reader's Digest Association, 1995.

de la Pena, Ramon S. *Upland Taro*. Department of Agricultural and Resource Economics, University of Hawai'i College of Tropical Agriculture, Home Garden Vegetable Series #18, November 1978.

Faust, Joan Lee. *The* New York Times *Book of Vegetable Gardening*. New York: Times Books, 1975.

Gilbert, J. C., and Yukio Nakagawa. *Tomatoes*. University of Hawai'i Cooperative Extension Service, Home Garden Vegetable Series #5, March 1978.

Hartman, Richard W. *"Poamoho" Pole Bean*. University of Hawai'i College of Tropical Agriculture, Research Extension Series 051, November, 1984.

Hartman, R. W., and Yukio Nakagawa. *Beans*. University of Hawai'i Cooperative Extension Service, Home Garden Vegetable Series #8, October 1978.

_____. *Edible-podded Pea*. University of Hawai'i Cooperative Extension Service, Home Garden Vegetable Series #11, October 1978.

_____. *Mustard Cabbage*. University of Hawai'i Cooperative Extension Service, Home Garden Vegetable Series #10, November 1978.

Hodge, Peggy Hickok. *Gardening in Hawai'i*. Honolulu: Mutual Publishing, 1996.

Joiner, Susan. *Grow Your Own Vegetables, Fruits and Herbs*. Secaucus, NJ: Chartwell Books, Inc., 1977.

McHugh, John J., Jr., and Steven K. Fukuda. *Hawaii Watercress Production*. University of Hawai'i College of Tropical Agriculture, Research Extension Series #099, December 1987.

Sato, Dale H. *Asparagus for the Home Garden*. University of Hawai'i Cooperative Extension Service, Horticulture, O'ahu Co. Leaflet #18, July 1981.

_____. *Tahitian Taro for the Home Garden*. University of Hawai'i Cooperative Extension Service, Horticulture, O'ahu Co. Leaflet #14, January 1981.

Sekioka, Terry T., and Kevin M. Yokoyama. *Irish Potatoes*. Department of Agricultural and Resource Economics, University of Hawai'i College of Tropical Agriculture, Home Garden Vegetable Series #9, March 1978.

Takeda, Kenneth Y. *Sweet Potato Production*. University of Hawai'i Cooperative Extension Service, Commodity Fact Sheet SP-3(A), September 1981.

Takeda, Kenneth Y., and Richard T. Sakuoka. *Onions: Bulb and Green Bunching Types*. University of Hawai'i Cooperative Extension Service, Home Garden Vegetable Series #16, January 1979.

_____. *Summer Squash*. University of Hawai'i Cooperative Extension Service, Home Garden Vegetable Series #15, November 1978.

Tanaka, Jack S., and Yukio Nakagawa. *Bell Pepper*. University of Hawai'i Cooperative Extension Service, Home Garden Vegetable Series #3, October 1978.

_____. *Cauliflower*. University of Hawai'i Cooperative Extension Service, Home Garden Vegetable Series #7, October 1978.

_____. *Sweet Potatoes*. University of Hawai'i Cooperative Extension Service, Home Garden Vegetable Series #12, March 1978.

Time-Life Encyclopedia of Gardening Vegetables and Fruits. New York: Time, Inc., 1972.

Western Garden Book. Menlo Park, CA: Sunset Publishing Corp., 1991.

UNIVERSITY OF HAWAI'I CTAHR AND EXTENSION SERVICE OFFICES

To obtrain a Seed Order Form from the University of Hawai'i CTAHR, write or call

Seed Program
University of Hawai'i, Department of Horticulture
3190 Maile Way, Room 112
Honolulu, HI 96822
Phone: (808) 956-7890
FAX: (808) 956-3894

UH EXTENSION SERVICE OFFICES:

HAWAI'I COUNTY

Hilo:

875 Komohana St.
Hilo, HI 96720
(808) 959-9155

Kamuela:

State Office Building
Kamuela, HI 96743
(808) 887-6183

Kona, Kainaliu:

P.O. Box 208
Kealakekua, HI 96750
(808) 322-2718

HONOLULU COUNTY

Kāne'ohe:

45-260 Waikalua Rd.
Kāne'ohe, HI 96744
(808) 247-0421

Wahiawā:

910 California Ave.
Wahiawā, HI 96786
(808) 622-4185

UH-Mānoa, Lower Campus:

1420 Lower Campus Rd.
Honolulu, HI 96822
(808) 948-7138

KAUA'I COUNTY

Līhue:

State Office Building
3060 Eiwa St.
Līhue, HI 96766
(808) 241-3471

MAUI COUNTY

Kahului, Maui:

310 Ka'ahumanu Ave. Bldg. 214
Kahului, HI 96732
(808) 244-3242

Kaunakakai, Moloka'i:

Ho'olehua Recreation Center
Kaunakakai, HI 96748
(808) 567-6833

NURSERIES AND SUPPLIERS

The following Hawai'i nurseries have a wide variety of plants and garden supplies, including the specialties listed.

HAWAI'I (BIG ISLAND)

Garden Exchange, Ltd.
300 Keawe St.
Hilo, HI 96720
(808) 961-2875 fax (808) 961-9234
U.H. seeds, asparagus, sweet potato, watercress, aloe, bamboo, breadfruit, pipinola, taro, and others

Hawaii True Value
19-4084 Old Volcano Rd.
Volcano, HI 96785
(808) 967-7969 fax (808) 985-7008
U.H. seeds, aloe

Hawaiian Gardens
Palani Rd. and Māmalahoa Hwy.
Kailua-Kona, HI 96745
(808) 329-5702 fax (808) 329-2082
asparagus, sweet potato, aloe, breadfruit tree, potato seeds, taro

Island Supply
30 Halekauila St.
Hilo, HI 96720
(808) 935-2881 fax (808) 969-1492
U.H. seeds, aloe, local varieties

Kapoho Kai Nursery
14-4790 La Nalo'o St.
Pāhoa, HI 96778
(808) 965-8839 fax (808) 965-7721

Quindembo Bamboo Nursery
P.O. Box 44556
Kawaihae, HI 96743
(808) 885-4968 fax (808) 885-4975
all types and varieties of bamboo

Rozett's Nursery
Left on 28th, off Kaloli Dr.
Hawaiian Paradise Park, Kea'au, HI 96749
(808) 982-5422 fax (808) 982-7763
aloe, bamboo, breadfruit, taro, and assorted vegetable starts

KAUA'I

Growing Greens Nursery
66-60 B Kawaihau Rd.
Kapa'a, HI 96746
(808) 822-3831 fax (same)
watercress, vegetable starts

Kaua'i Nursery and Landscaping
3-1550 Kaumuali'i Hwy.
Līhu'e, HI 96766
(808) 245-7747 toll-free: (888) 345-7747 fax (808) 245-9289
e-mail: knl@gte.net website: http://planet-hawaii.com/hawaii-express
sweet potato, aloe, bamboo, breadfruit tree, taro, assorted vegetable starts

Lawai Valley Nursery
4951 Kua Rd. (P.O. Box 252)
Kalaheo, HI 96741
(808) 332-7772
aloe, breadfruit tree, taro

MAUI

Ka Lima O Maui Plant Nursery
95 Mahalani St.
Wailuku, HI 96793
(808) 244-7093 fax (808) 244-2077
aloe

Kula Ace Hardware and Nursery
735 Lower Kula Rd. (P.O. Box 539)
Kula, HI 96790
(808) 878-2551 fax (808) 878-2427
U.H. seeds, asparagus, sweet potato, watercress, aloe, breadfruit, pipinola, potato, taro

O'AHU

Frankie's Nursery
41-999 Mahiku Pl.
Waimānalo, HI 96795
(808) 259-8737 fax (808)259-8737
breadfruit trees

The Garden House
1213 S. Beretania St.
Honolulu, HI 96814
(808) 596-2117 fax (808) 596-2118
U.H. seeds, asparagus, sweet potato,
watercress, aloe, bamboo, breadfruit,
pipinola, potato, taro

Kahua Nurseries, Inc.
91-2002 Fort Weaver Road
Ewa Beach, HI 96706
(808) 681-5664 fax (808) 681-5663
U.H. seeds, asparagus, aloe, taro

Kilgo Co. Inc.
180 Sand Island Rd.
Honolulu, HI 96819
(808) 832-2200 fax (808) 832-2201
U.H. seeds

Mokuleia Landscape and Nursery
Co.
68-415 Kikou St.
Waialua, HI 96791
(808) 637-1670 fax (808) 637-1670
aloe, breadfruit tree, taro

Oka Nursery
333 Aoloa St. #312
Kailua, HI 96734
(808) 263-6094 Fax (808) 261-8092
aloe, taro

R and S Nursery
938 Kamilonui Pl.
Honolulu, HI 96825
(808) 395-9811 fax (808) 395-7912
aloe, breadfruit tree

Sharon's Plants Ltd.
41-614 Waikupanaha St.
Waimānalo, HI 96795
(808) 259-7173 fax (808) 259-9564
breadfruit tree

SUPPLIERS

Bamboo:
Quindembo Bamboo Nursery
P.O. Box 44556
Kawaihae, HI 96743
Ph: (808) 885-4968
FAX: (808) 885-4975

Hawaiian Moon Calendar:
Prince Kūhiō Hawaiian Civic
Club
P.O. Box 240132
Honolulu, HI 96824

Mainland Seed Companies:
Although disease-resistant seeds
developed by the University of
Hawai'i are highly recommended
for the Hawai'i vegetable gardener,
the following are good sources of
seeds not available from UH:

W. Atlee Burpee Co.
300 Park Ave.
Warminster, PA 18974
Write for free catalog.

Filaree Farm
Route 1
Okanogan, WA 98840
Write for catalog.

Nichols Garden Nursery
1190 N. Pacific Highway
Albany, OR 97321
Write for free catalog.

Park Seed Company
Cokesbury Road
Greenwood, S.C. 29647
Write for free catalog.

Peters Seed and Research
407 Maranatha Lane
Myrtle Creek, OR 97457
Catalog costs $2.00.

Pinetree Garden Seeds
P.O. Box 300
Rte. 100
New Gloucester, ME 04260
Write for free catalog.

Shepherd's Garden Seeds
6116 Highway 9
Felton, CA 95018
Write for free catalog.

RECIPE INDEX

ABOUT THE AUTHOR

Kathy Oshiro grew up on an acre of land in Southern California, where she learned to appreciate the joys and advantages, both physical and psychological, of working the soil. While attending California State University-Humboldt and working for the federal government, she owned a five-acre farm, where she raised beef cattle, goats, laying hens, and vegetables.

When she moved to Maui in January 1979, she discovered that living in Hawai'i allowed her to have vegetables in her garden year-round. After three years in Upcountry Maui, she moved to Lāna'i, where working in her backyard vegetable garden taught her soil improvement techniques as well as methods for combating drought conditions and unwanted insects.

After eleven years on Lāna'i, she and her family moved to the Big Island, where they now have a 28-acre farm. They raise grass-fed sheep, using rotational grazing methods, and are exploring several diversified agriculture alternatives, including maile, bamboo, coffee, and 'awa.

When she is not working in her garden, cooking, or reading cookbooks, Kathy assists her husband, Glenn, with a website, smallfarms.com, designed to help small farmers and ranchers nationwide market more directly to consumers. True to small family farm tradition, her daughters also lend a hand in this project.